Great Ideas For
Primary
Activity Days

Great Ideas For
Primary
Activity Days

by
Trina Boice

spring creek
BOOK COMPANY

Provo, Utah

ISBN: 978-1-932898-69-9
e. 1

Published by:
Spring Creek Book Company
P.O. Box 50355
Provo, Utah 84605-0355

www.springcreekbooks.com

Cover design © Spring Creek Book Company
Cover design by Nicole Cunningham

Printed in the United States of America
10 9 8 7 6 5 4 3 2 1
Printed on acid-free paper

Library of Congress Cataloging-in-Publication Data

Boice, Trina, 1963-
  Great ideas for Primary Activity Day / by Trina Boice.
     p. cm.
  ISBN 978-1-932898-69-9 (pbk. : alk. paper)
  1. Christian education of children. 2. Christian education--Activity
programs. 3. Church of Jesus Christ of Latter-day Saints--Education. I.
Title.

BX8610.B65 2007
268.432088289332--dc22
                                                    2006100032

Table of Contents

Chapter One

Welcome to Activity Day

Remember the conversation Jesus had with Peter when the counsel was given to "feed my sheep"? (John 21:15-17) You may have noticed that before Jesus asked His beloved disciple to take care of His sheep He said, "feed my lambs." Now, that may seem like unimportant wording, but to me it sends the message that we need to care for and teach our littlest ones first. They are not to be overlooked in God's kingdom here on earth. We are to nurture them physically and spiritually.

During the first 48 years of the history of the LDS Church the children did not have their own organization. Aurelia Spencer Rogers was a mother of 12 children, and she was concerned about the rowdy behavior of the boys in the neighborhood. She spoke with Eliza R. Snow, the General Relief Society President at the time, who then mentioned it to the prophet, John Taylor. Sister Rogers asked if the little boys could have their own organization where they could be "trained to make better men."

The prophet liked the idea, but he thought such an organization would be better if the little girls were also included. He thought the girls would make the singing sound better!

Sister Rogers was called to be the first Primary President and in 1878 the first Primary meeting was held in Farmington, Utah, with 215 boys and girls "to be taught obedience, faith in God, prayer, punctuality, and good manners." (*Encyclopedia of Mormonism,* 5 vols. 1992, 3:1146)

Over the years the Primary program has evolved, but the purpose has always been the same: to "teach children the gospel

1

of Jesus Christ and help them learn to live it." (*Church Handbook of Instructions, Book 2: Priesthood and Auxiliary Leaders* 1998, 229)

This purpose is based on 3 Nephi 22:13, which reads, "And all thy children shall be taught of the Lord; and great shall be the peace of thy children."

The eighth General Primary President, Michaelene P. Grassli, counseled, "When children are taught of the Lord we bestow on them a gift, a legacy of peace that can lead them to eternal life. We must not fail them." (April 2003 Open House)

To have faith in God is to have peace. Today, the Faith in God program is the gift of peace we can give our children in a turbulent world.

In addition to working on goals in the Faith of God program, Activity Days should provide our Primary children opportunities to:

- Learn the gospel and practice living it
- Develop good habits at an early age
- Build gospel-centered friendships
- Participate in missionary work by inviting their friends to a fun activity
- Prepare for the transition into the Young Men and Young Women's programs
- Prepare for receiving the priesthood
- Develop a testimony
- Develop and share talents
- Learn how to keep the covenants made at baptism
- Serve others
- Be prepared to make good choices
- Come unto Christ

Remember to open and close your Activity Day with prayer. The purpose of the activities is not to just have activities, but to develop faith in God! We live in perilous times when attacks on the family have become quite aggressive. We need to be able to fight back harder and protect the Savior's lambs. While Satan has had thousands of years to develop his destroying powers, the young children whom we are called to protect and nurture have lived less than a dozen years here on earth and are ill-prepared to protect themselves alone. We need to equip them with tools, dress them with spiritual armor and surround them with love and safety.

In 1979, President Ezra Taft Benson said:

"For nearly six thousand years, God has held you in reserve to make your appearance in the final days before the second coming of the Lord. Every previous gospel dispensation has drifted into apostasy, but ours will not. While our generation will be comparable in wickedness to the days of Noah, when the Lord cleansed the earth by flood, there is a major difference this time.

"It is that God has saved for the final inning some of his strongest children who will help bear off the kingdom triumphantly. And that is where you come in, for you are the generation that must be prepared to meet your God. All through the ages the prophets have looked down through the corridors of time to our day. Billions of the deceased and those yet to be born have their eyes on us.

"Make no mistake about it-you are a marked generation. There has never been more expected of the faithful in such a short period of time as there is of us. Never before on the face of this earth have the forces of evil and the forces of good been as well organized.

"Now is the great day of the devil's power, with the greatest mass murderers of all time living among us. But now is also the great day of the Lord's power, with the greatest number ever of priesthood holders on the earth. And the showdown is fast approaching." (Provo, Utah: BYU Press, 1980, p.59)

When you are set apart as a Primary Activity Day leader you are given a mantel of authority and the right to receive personal revelation for those whom you serve. Pray to understand the needs of the children. Every girl is unique and it will be your challenge to touch her life and her heart. To be an effective leader you will need to know her and understand her challenges.

Prepare yourself in every way as you invite His precious daughters to "come unto Christ." The most important thing you will do is to introduce them to Him and help them want to be more like Him. As you are prayerful and diligent, many ways to impact and touch their lives will be opened to you.

One thing I learned very quickly on my mission is that my words were not as important as I thought they were. I had competed on the Speech & Debate team for four years during my college years at BYU, so when I went on my mission to Spain I tried very hard to learn the correct vocabulary words I thought would have the most impact.

I soon realized that it wasn't my word choice that converted souls to Christ, but rather, the testifying power of the Holy Ghost! The most important thing I could do was to create an environment where the Holy Ghost would be welcome and could touch the heart of the listener. That is your challenge as a Primary worker as well.

You can spend hours planning lessons or activities, but if the children aren't opening up their scriptures and supping from its pages with you, they won't go home filled spiritually. Help them to love the scriptures and learn how to pray.

Those are two things that will strengthen and nourish their faith for the rest of their lives. Create a loving, supportive, safe environment for your girls so their hearts will be softened and receptive to the testifying witness of the Holy Ghost. More important than feeling their leaders' love, the children must feel the Savior's love.

When I was a little girl in Primary I had many teachers who inspired me to be good by their teaching, but more importantly, by their actions. They helped me learn how to apply the gospel to my life and gave me opportunities to practice. I remember one summer day when my sweet teacher was teaching a lesson about the Word of Wisdom. Instead of simply presenting gospel principles and ending the lesson with a prayer, she handed each one of us a 3 x 5 card where upon we were to write our commitment to live the law. I still have that card!

Throughout my life, whenever I have been in a situation requiring I make a decision about whether or not to drink alcohol, take drugs, or smoke, I have easily been able to choose the right because those choices were already made by me in a small Primary room years ago with the help of an inspired Primary teacher. I don't remember her name, but I'll never forget how she taught me the gospel, as well as how to live it.

Let the girls know you love the Lord and find joy in living the gospel. Provide them with opportunities to practice living the gospel and see how to apply it to their lives daily as they make choices, go to school, spend time with friends, and live at home. Help them to transfer their understanding of the gospel from their head to their heart. While preparing your lessons and activities, prayerfully consider the girls' needs. You are not teaching lessons; you are teaching Heavenly Father's children!

Before reading this book you should first become very familiar with the material the Church has provided you for your calling, such as the Faith in God booklet, *The Friend* magazine, leadership manuals, and the Church's web site (www.lds.org).

This book has been organized simply—it follows along with the Faith in God booklet, page by page. At the end of this book are additional chapters filled with fun ideas to incorporate into your ward or branch. Every unit of the Church has its own unique personality and needs, so feel free to tweak the ideas to meet the needs of your own Primary. Remember that children thrive when given a mixture of fun and inspirational activities.

Whether you serve in the Primary program for a few months or a few years, you will grow closer to the Savior as you develop pure love for His lambs. One of my favorite passages of scripture tells when the Savior appeared to the Nephites and commanded that their little children should be brought to Him. (3 Nephi 17:11-25).

There must have been many children in that multitude, and yet Christ took the time to bless them one by one and pray for them. That is a powerful lesson—each soul is rescued one at a time.

My heart fills with wonder and love as I try to imagine what it would have been like to see the angels descend from heaven in the midst of fire, encircling those little ones about, ministering to them. Today, you are the angel who has been called to minister to the Lord's littlest ones in His kingdom. May you share His love and gospel with them and be blessed for your faithful service.

Chapter Two

I Am a Child of God

Every Primary child quickly learns the words to the classic Primary song "I Am a Child of God." The activity ideas for the first page of the Faith in God booklet are to help transfer those words from the tongue into the heart of each child. Plan a day when you can take photos of each of the children to place in their Faith In God booklets. Also, talk about the words on the inside cover page of their booklet and incorporate some of the following ideas into your activities to help the children really internalize those words.

- Go on a hike and talk about all the beautiful things the Lord has created, including the girls themselves!

- Have a progressive dinner where the girls start in one home eating appetizers, then go to another house for salad, then another house for the entrée and to a final house for dessert. At each home have a short lesson on various aspects of their divine nature and compare the progressive dinner to our progression back to our heavenly home.

- Learn about the song "I Am a Child of God" and its composer, Naomi W. Randall. Teach the girls how to conduct it and coordinate an opportunity for them to do so during Sharing Time on Sunday. Learn to sing it in another language.

- Introduce the girls to new LDS musicians by playing their music when appropriate during your meetings. Write letters or e-mails to the artists to thank them for sharing their talents and musical testimonies.

- Decorate purses, backpacks, canvas shoes, jeans, or T-shirts to help the girls remember who they are and whose they are.

- Learn how to make different kinds of candles and talk about what it means to "wax strong" like in the scriptures.

- Talk about nature and the Lord's handiwork, emphasizing that we are His greatest creation. Teach the girls various kinds of "handiwork" such as crocheting, cross-stitch, knitting, and tatting. Have them write "I Am a Child of God" on their project, using a new stitch they have learned.

- Talk about how the Church magazines help us remember who we are. Spend time sharing stories and projects from *The Friend* magazine.

- Go to a local planetarium and learn about this incredible universe Heavenly Father has created for us! Many local colleges have free shows and observatories you could visit. Talk about how each girl plays an important part in the plan.

- Talk about their "sweet" spirits and teach them how to make their own perfume, mixing different oils and fragrances. Have them design a name and logo for their creation.

- Hold a "Tacky Night" where everyone comes dressed in tacky clothes, eats tacky food. Then talk about how to dress and behave in a "classy" manner that is becoming of someone who truly has divinity within them.

- Make cute photo albums using different kinds of styles, and then talk about how important their lives are to Heavenly Father. Show some scrapbooking techniques as well.

- Decorate journals and talk about how writing can be therapeutic, enabling us to see our potential and remember we are children of a loving Heavenly Father.

- Talk about what a blessing our families are. Share ideas on Family Home Evening lessons. Prepare a lesson the girls could use next week at home with their families, including visual aids, refrigerator magnets and recipes for refreshments.

- Read *The Velveteen Rabbit* and talk about the "real" worth of each girl. Learn how to sew fabric bunnies.

- Teach the girls about Family History and talk about how we inherit physical and personality traits from our parents. Help them create a photo pedigree chart for their family. Then talk about the traits we receive from our heavenly parents.

- Have the girls create a poster or bulletin board to display in the Primary room that reminds all of the children that they are each a child of God.

- Encourage the girls to help one another identify why they are special by having them write down positive character traits they see in others. Pass around a piece of paper with each girl's name on it and take turns writing and passing the papers around until everyone's page is full of kind words.

- Invite the Young Women in your ward to share with your Primary girls what they know about one of the values in the Young Women's program called "Divine Nature." They are sure to have lots of great ideas!

- Cut out paper letters that spell "I Am a Child of God" and hide them around the room. Invite the girls to find the letters and figure out what it spells. Talk about how sometimes it takes a lot of searching for some people to realize how valued they are.

- Sit in a circle and play music while the girls pass a mirror around. When the music stops, the girl holding the mirror looks at her reflection and tells one way that Heavenly Father shows His love for His children.

- Watch the video or read the story *The Princess and the Pea*. Talk about how each girl is a daughter of a heavenly king! Make tiaras or decorate crowns from Burger King.

- Show photos of baby animals with adult animals and see if the girls know what the babies are called. Talk about how they are like their Heavenly Father.

- Put a light behind each girl's head to shine onto black paper and draw their profile with a white marker.

- Paint and decorate clothespins to look like girls. Talk about how each clothespin is unique and special, just like the girls are.

Chapter Three

First Presidency Letter

- Read the First Presidency Letter together and show pictures of the current First Presidency. Talk about each of the men, sharing stories from their lives that can be found in the *Ensign* by doing a search at www.lds.org.

- Explain what a presidency is and how it works. Use your Primary presidency as an example.

- Put a blanket on the floor, munch on snacks and watch the July 2002 video entitled "Sharing Time With President Gordon B. Hinckley" or the February 8, 2003 broadcast entitled "The 125th Anniversary of Primary" featuring President Hinckley. Your ward library should have access to these videos.

- Write a letter to the First Presidency, thanking them for all they do for the children of the world. Send cards and letters to:

    The Church of Jesus Christ of Latter-day Saints
    Church Office Building
    First Presidency
    50 E. North Temple
    Salt Lake City, Utah 84150

- Use pictures of latter-day prophets and apostles and play "Concentration" so the girls can become more familiar with their faces. Photos of the First Presidency and Twelve Apostles can be found at http://lds.about.com_library_bl_games_apostlecards2.pdf

- Sing the Primary song "Follow The Prophet" and have the girls create original verses for some of the latter-day prophets.

- Share with the girls what some of the prophets were like when they were young by reading stories from the book *Boys Who Became Prophets* by Lynda Cory Hardy.

- Teach the girls how to sing "We Thank Thee, Oh God, For A Prophet" and coordinate a date with your ward leaders when the girls could sing it in Sacrament Meeting or during Sharing Time.

- Assign each girl a different modern-day prophet or apostle to learn about. Have her bring a picture and teach the others about him at your next gathering.

- Teach the girls how to make some of the prophets' favorite recipes such as Joseph Fielding Smith's sherbet, Harold B. Lee's boiled raisin cake, Spencer W. Kimball's raspberry cheesecake, Ezra Taft Benson's lemon meringue pie or Wilford Woodruff's cherry nut cake.

- Find out when the current prophet's birthday is and send him a special card that the girls make for him.

Chapter Four

My Baptismal Covenant

Have the girls take turns reading each line of the Church-produced sheet "My Baptismal Covenant" that is given in most stakes to newly baptized members. Try some of the following ideas to help them gain a greater understanding and appreciation for the promises that were made on their baptismal day:

- Invite the missionaries to speak to the girls about how they teach investigators and prepare them for baptism. Encourage the girls to share experiences of baptisms they have attended.
- Talk about being physically and spiritually clean. Create special soaps by placing paper designs on bars of white soap and dipping the top into melted wax.
- Help them memorize "My Baptismal Covenant" by playing games that review and test their learning. Write it on a chalkboard and slowly erase one word at a time while they learn each line.
- Learn about different people in the scriptures who have been baptized. Study the experience of Alma and the people who were baptized in the Waters of Mormon. Make puppets, flannel figures or visual aids so the girls could share the stories with their families during Family Home Evening.
- Create a slide-show presentation that could be shown at a baptismal service while the person getting baptized is changing out of his/her wet clothing. The girls could be recorded singing Primary songs to be played during the presentation.

- Have the children share special feelings about their baptisms. Create baptism scrapbook pages if they haven't made any yet.
- Make gifts and cards that the children could give to other children who will be getting baptized soon, such as white towels or socks, frames, bags or journals. Some cute poems that could go with the gifts can be found at http://www.theideadoor.com/Baptism.html
- Get a list from your Primary presidency of the children who will be getting baptized in the next year and their birthdates. Plan to attend their baptisms together as a class. Prepare folders with information, word games, baptism puzzles and other material to help prepare the children for baptism. Present the folders to the children who will be getting baptized within the next year.
- Learn a song that the girls could sing at someone's baptism. If any of the girls play a musical instrument, try to incorporate those talents into your musical number.
- Have the girls make Family Home Evening packets to take home that include a lesson about baptism, visual aids, refrigerator magnets, recipes for refreshments and suggested scripture verses and songs to sing.
- Draw pictures about baptism that could be used as artwork to be displayed at a baptism or used on the written program.
- Contact your stake leader in charge of baptismal services and arrange to clean the baptismal font together in preparation for your ward's next baptism.
- Prepare a special Sharing Time presentation for your Primary about the importance of baptism and the covenants that are made.
- Invite an attorney to explain to the girls about contracts, promises, and covenants in simple terms, as well as talk about what happens in court when they are broken.
- Have the girls make bookmarks or door hangers for their bedrooms with the words from "My Baptismal Covenant." If you use glow-in-the-dark paint, the girls will be reminded of the words even after their bedroom lights go out!

- Learn where our latter-day prophets were baptized by reviewing the article "Our Prophets' Places of Baptism" in the August 1997 issue of *The Friend*.

- Watch "Baptism–A Promise To Follow Jesus" as a group. (Primary Video Collection #53179).

- Play the fun Finch Family Game "Fill The Font."

- Prepare inexpensive baptism gifts that the girls could give to new converts in your ward.

- Create an ornament or bookmark which has a picture of the Savior being baptized on one side and a picture of each girl standing in front of the baptismal font in your Church building.

- Teach the girls how to make a bracelet with white beads and talk about the symbolism of white.

- Invite some Young Men to share their thoughts on the Aaronic Priesthood and the importance of the Sacrament.

Chapter Five

Award Requirements

Basic Requirements

Pray daily to Heavenly Father.

- Talk about the importance of prayer and share stories about people who had their prayers answered.
- Study the Lord's prayer found in Matthew 6:9-13.
- Teach the girls how to pray, using proper language.
- Learn how to sing and conduct Primary songs about prayer. Teach them a song in sign language or another tongue.
- Go online to learn about the history of the pretzel and how it relates to prayer. Teach the girls how to make home-made pretzels and taste them with different kinds of mustard.
- Decorate pillow cases by writing the gospel standards with fabric ink.
- Make prayer dolls that the girls can keep on their bed to remind them to pray. A cute and simple pattern can be found at http://www.netw.com/~rafter4/nettie.htm
- Make "Prayer Rocks." You can find several different poems online to go with them.
- Add hair and a face to a square block of wood. Teach them to remember the four steps of prayer by showing them the four sides of a square: Dear Heavenly Father, We Thank Thee, We Ask Thee, In the Name of Jesus Christ.

- Show pictures of Joseph Smith, Jr. in the Sacred Grove. Read James 1:5 and have the girls draw a picture or write down specific questions they'd like to ask Heavenly Father about.

- Have a PJs party: Prayer, Journal, Scriptures. Have a modest pajamas fashion show and make crafts that remind the girls of the things they need to do before they go to sleep each night.

- Help the girls write a letter to Heavenly Father and talk about how prayer is like writing a letter to someone we know and love.

- Teach the girls how to make rag rugs with strips of cloth that they can put on the floor next to their bed to remind them to pray. Check out http://www.netw.com/~rafter4/article.htm

- Present her with her very own Prayer Bear. Oriental Trading Company is great for inexpensive gifts. Before ordering online do a Google search for "coupon code" for the store and you can save on shipping or a percentage off your order. You can also order by phone at 1-800-875-8480 or 1-800-228-2269. Include this poem:

I'm just a little Prayer Bear,
I'll sit upon your bed.
It's my job to remind you
When your prayers should be said.

When you put me on your pillow
As you make your bed each day,
Remember as you hold me,
To take the time to pray.

Then when you go to bed at night
And put me on the floor,
Remember to take the time to kneel
And say your prayers once more.

- Make prayer rugs by stenciling designs or words on free carpet store samples with fabric paint.

- Make those old-fashioned tin can telephones with a string attached and see if the girls can hear each other when talking. Compare talking on a phone to prayer.

- Give each girl a rope and tell her to make a knot without letting go of each end. They won't be able to do it (but it will be entertaining to watch them try!) Now, have them fold their arms like they're going to pray. Give each girl a rope again and tell her to pull each end. The knot will form easily! Talk about how, with prayer, impossible tasks can be accomplished and when life gets crazy to hang on!

- Invite the missionaries to share how they teach investigators to pray, as well as some inspiring stories they have witnessed on their missions regarding prayer.

- Decorate a gratitude journal where the girls could record the blessings they're grateful for. Challenge them to offer a prayer without asking for anything.

- Each girl decorates a popsickle stick with her name on it. Each time you open and close your Activity Day have the person saying the prayer choose a stick out of a container to include the name of that girl in her prayer.

- Present each girl with a prayer necklace from Lowman & Co. along with the poem that reminds them to pray.

- Make simple lion puppets and share the story of Daniel in the lions' den.

- Make pioneer bonnets or skirts and share some of the stories of pioneers who had their prayers answered.

Read the scriptures regularly.

- Make bookmarks by laminating pressed flowers or attaching ribbons or a picture of the Savior to a card each girl designs.

- Make sock puppets or marionettes the girls could use to act out scripture stories.

- Create a small chart that could be kept with each girl's scriptures where she could check off each day she remembers to read the scriptures.

- Draw the head of a scripture character, leaving a hole in the middle for the girls to put their faces in. The girls wear their "masks" and act out the story.

- Play scripture charades or Pictionary.

- Begin a R.E.D. program with the girls! Take turns bringing something RED to share with each other each time to remind everyone to Read Every Day!

- There are tons of fun recipes online for scripture cake, cookies and bread you could make so the girls can really sink their teeth into the scriptures! The ingredients are found within scripture verses.

- Help the girls think harder about the scriptures in a fun way. Divide the girls into small teams and provide each group a set of scriptures and scripture reference clues that will direct them to various stores in the mall. Meet at the food court for refreshments.

- Find all of the scriptures that talk about light. Light candles outside and take turns trying to extinguish them with squirt guns. Talk about how we can follow the Savior's light, as well as reflect it.

- Make shrink art by cutting a piece of heavy plastic into the shape of objects or people in the scriptures, or even the scriptures themselves. Draw on the plastic with permanent markers and punch a hole in one end of the shape so the design can be turned into a necklace or bracelet or bookmark dangle. Lay the plastic on foil-covered sheets and heat in a warm oven until the designs shrink!

- Talk about various people in the scriptures who encountered rough water, such as Noah, Jonah, and Lehi's family. Create a course the girls have to ride on with a tricycle or on roller blades while the other girls shoot water on them with squirt guns.

- Each girl receives one bead for each day she reads the scriptures. By the end of the month she should have enough to make a pretty bracelet or necklace. Teach them how to make jewelry. Simple kits can be purchased at Michaels, Target or Wal-Mart.

- Talk about how Christ invited the disciples to become "fishers of men" and have the girls learn how to fish or play one of those fishing carnival-type games.

- Have the girls share their favorite scripture with one another and create a special wall hanging, bookmark or door hanger with it. If you use glow-in-the-dark paint the girls will be reminded to read the scriptures each night before they go to sleep!

- Decorate calendars at the beginning of a new year. Teach them how to create their own stickers to use for each day they remember to read their scriptures. They have sticker-making machines at Wal-Mart and Michaels.

- Help the girls memorize the monthly scriptures recited in Primary during the theme.

- Listen to pretty music while the girls mark their scriptures, using Seminary Scripture Mastery verses or the ones used in missionary discussions, or any others of their choosing.

- Draw a map of Church history sites, Book of Mormon lands or Bible cities on a plastic tarp or tablecloth and have the girls throw wet sponges on certain places as you read the scriptures mentioning them.

- Discuss the travels of famous missionaries in the scriptures (Paul, Alma the Younger and the sons of Mosiah) and create a maze or obstacle course.

- Ask girls to find a scripture about a particular topic or one that uses a specific word. When they do they get to shoot a basket or throw a wadded up paper ball into a waste basket. Top score wins.

- Choose one of the books in the Bible (or other scriptures) to be the clue for Hangman. The girls can ask Yes or No questions. Each time the answer is No you draw another element on the hangman until they can guess the book.

- Invite a Seminary teacher to share some of the wonderful things her class is learning this year. (Seminary teachers are very creative!)

- Watch a video about a particular scripture story. There are dozens of animated, dramatic, and even musical versions to be found in LDS and Christian bookstores!

- Challenge the girls to write their own parable and share it with one another by acting it out or reading their story.

- Teach the girls how to bake bread and talk about the wise counsel "Man shall not live by bread alone, but by every word that proceedeth out of the mouth of God."

- Decorate journals the girls could write in to record impressions they feel while reading the scriptures each night.

- Munch on goodies while listening to the scriptures on CD or cassette tapes.

- Show the girls how to prepare "glue-ins" for them to put into their scriptures. A glue-in is a small picture with a quote from a prophet or Apostle that adds insight to a particular scripture verse.

- Bring a tape recorder and have the girls record their favorite scripture passages that could then be given to the older members in your ward who have trouble reading.

- Create illustrations to go with certain scripture stories.

- Take a field trip to your Church's library and you'll surely find some hidden gems: flannel board scripture stories, videos, "Scripture Readers", pictures and tons more!

- Decorate the room with cars and traffic signs and theme the activity "Route 66." Talk about what's inside each of the 66 books in the Bible and how the scriptures are like a roadmap for our lives. Have the girls make Pinewood Derby cars!

- Decorate little boxes of raisins to look like scriptures by placing black construction paper slightly over the edges of a gold-painted raisin box. Attach a little ribbon before you glue everything down and decorate the top to look like any of the Standard Works.

- Find mention of different kinds of food in the scripture and taste them, such as figs, dates, leavened bread, fish, fruit, etc.

- Prepare a special etiquette dinner and talk about feasting on the words of Christ.

Keep the commandments and live "my gospel standards."

- Learn how to cross stitch by creating a wall hanging or pillow, using the gospel standards.
- Talented musician, Tara Tarbet, has composed music for each of the standards to help children learn and internalize them! For free copies of the sheet music check out: http://www.mormonmomma.com/mini/gsmusic.html
- Using the items from "My Gospel Standards" play charades or Pictionary.
- Make door hangers with the gospel standards written on them.
- Using glow-in-the-dark paint, write the gospel standards on a wood plaque that can be hung up in each girl's bedroom so she will be able to see the words at night as she drifts off to sleep.
- Find another group of Activity Day girls in the world who would like to be Pen Pals. Share letters, pictures and care packages, and talk about how they are living the commandments and "My Gospel Standards." Join an online discussion group (see Web Sites chapter) to find Primary leaders who would be interested in forming such a Pen Pal friendship with your ward.
- Have a modesty fashion show, using newspaper and duct tape to create outfits the girls will wear down a runway. Award silly prizes for "Most Creative", "Most stylish", etc.
- Choose one of the items in "My Gospel Standards" to focus on each month. Because there are 13 of them you'll have to double up one month.
- Make paper dolls or puppets that the girls can dress modestly and do various role play scenarios.
- Make Shrink Art designs using gospel-oriented objects.
- For a page of small "My Gospel Standards" cards that could be cut out and colored by the girls, click on "Sharing Time" http://www.lds.org/churchmagazines/6-2006-Friend/Jun2006Friend.pdf
- Invite "Moses" to attend your Activity Day so that your girls could interview him and learn about the Ten Commandments.

- Bake cookies into the shape of numbers and talk about each of the Ten Commandments.
- Decorate a poster or bulletin board in the Primary room to remind all of the children about "My Gospel Standards."
- Invite the missionaries to explain how they teach the commandments and standards of the Church to their investigators.
- Have the girls fill prescription bottles with candy and talk about how the gosPILL is the best kind of medicine!
- Play different kinds of recitation games to help the girls memorize the 13 lines. For some memorizing tricks check out www.memoryverses.org/tricks.htm
- Make mobiles for the girls' bedrooms using 13 elements to represent each line in "My Gospel Standards."
- Shape Kool-Aid Playdough into gospel-oriented designs:
    3 cups flour
    ½ cup salt
    2 Kool-Aid packages
    2 cups boiling water

  Mix dry ingredients together and then add boiling water. Knead on a floured board and then play!

Honor your parents and be kind to your family.

- Bake cookies together that the girls can take home to their families.
- Have the girls make candy-gram messages for their families.
- Invite the girls to bring lots of different kinds of stickers and stationery to write thank you notes to their families.
- Help the girls decorate "Kindness Cans" they will share with their families. Each time someone sees a family member do something kind he/she writes it down on a slip of paper to put in the can or jar to be read at next week's Family Home Evening.
- Teach the girls how to make and decorate gingerbread houses during the holidays. Talk about what they can do to make their real homes more sweet.

- There are dozens of recipes online to make lip balm inexpensively. Decorate film canisters or other small containers to put the lip balm in. Talk about the importance of having kind words leave our lips.

- Have the girls make decorative gift bags out of lunch bags. Fill them with treats and have the girls present one to each member of her family with a note that says, "Having you in my family is sweet!"

- Make sticky buns and have the girls take some home with a note that says, "A loving family STICKS together!"

- Celebrate "Respect For Parents Day" on August 1st. Check out some fun craft ideas at www.dltk-holidays.com

- Make some kind of a Family Home Evening task chart or board the girls can use each week at home to remember who is in charge of the lesson, prayer, refreshments, etc.

- Teach the girls how to frame a nice copy of "The Family: A Proclamation To The World" to hang in their bedrooms or homes.

- Talk about fun family traditions and invite each girl to share with the group some of the things her family does.

- Using cardboard boxes, create "houses" and display a picture of each person in the family in a different window. Fill the box with goodies the girls can share with their families.

- Choose a nice location or backdrop and invite the families to have their pictures taken by someone in your ward with some photography talent.

- Help the girls create a Coat of Arms for their family to display by designing their own or searching for their historic one. See www.yourchildlearns.com/heraldry.htm

- Visit your closest Family History Center to learn more about genealogy.

- Help the girls print family trees that display their pedigree in a beautiful way. You can make your own or even buy one online where you get to choose from a variety of frames, styles, sizes, backgrounds and fancy paper.

- Create Christmas ornaments by using mini frames with family photos inside or by making special ornaments out of quilted pieces of special fabric used for weddings, baby blankets, or another special event.

- Decoupage boxes, benches, or even dressers by using copies of special photographs, drawings or other cutouts that have special meaning to the family's history.

- Build or create a special trunk where family history items can be stored.

- Make quilts or pillows using photos that have been transferred to fabric.

- Help the girls design a calendar using family photos for each month. Include birthdates of important ancestors and other special family history events.

- Using copies of the girls' family photographs or drawings, design greeting cards.

- Show the girls how to make their own diaries by using copies of pictures of ancestors to design the front cover and illustrate other pages throughout the book.

- Using the kind of poster paper that comes on rolls, have each girl make a time-line of her family's history.

- Show the girls how to draw and laminate placemats for her family to use.

- Decorate frames with buttons, silk flowers, or other small items for the girls to keep a family photo in.

- Using calligraphy, create a framed picture with each girl's family name and try to learn the historic meaning of that name. Check out www.last-names.net/Articles/Anatomy.asp

- Show the girls how to create a family party book where they write down all of the things their family does throughout the year to celebrate holidays, birthdays, anniversaries, baptisms, any other special occasions.

- Invite each girl to find out her "culinary heritage" and bring a dish to share with the others that represents her ancestors' home country.

- Invite each girl's grandparents to share an Activity Day together and celebrate "Grandparents Day."
- Help the girls create funny anagrams, using the names of each member in their family to be shared at Family Home Evening.
- Teach the girls how to make paper dolls or puppets to resemble each family member.
- Introduce the girls to the beautiful music on "Divinity of the Family" at www.ldsounds.com
- Help the girls make special gifts for Grandparents Day (first Sunday after Labor Day each year.) Check out some cute ideas at www.dltk-kids.com/crafts/grandparents/index.html

Pay your tithing and attend tithing settlement.

- Buy inexpensive piggy banks and have the girls decorate them while you talk about tithing.
- Create special boxes with three dividers: one for tithing, one for savings, and one for spending money. Talk about the importance of each area of money management.
- Show the girls how to fill out a tithing slip. Invite one of the Bishopric members or clerk to talk about what happens to the envelope and funds after they receive it.
- Teach the girls about Lorenzo Snow and the revelation on tithing.
- Share uplifting stories about the blessings of tithing.
- Help the girls prepare a Family Home Evening lesson about tithing that they could share with their families.
- If you're lucky enough to live near a Bishop's Storehouse or Home Storage Center, take a field trip and talk about how tithes and fast offerings help the poor.
- Invite the Bishop to talk to the girls about tithing settlement and what to expect when they come into his office with their families in December.
- Each girl brings candy pieces to count out and practice figuring out ten percent for tithing. Talk about how paying our tithing brings sweet rewards.

Attend Sacrament Meeting and Primary regularly.

- Decorate a special jar the girls can put a small item in (marble, silk flower, etc) to represent each time they attend their Church meetings. When the jar is full the group can get a special treat.

- Teach the girls how to bake bread and make some for next Sunday's Sacrament Meeting.

- Help the girls prepare a "Sunday Bag" where they will keep their scriptures, pictures of Jesus, gospel coloring books, *The Friend* magazine, and other things they can quietly look at during Sacrament Meeting to help them be reverent. A large collection of clip art and coloring pages can be found at the website www.jennysmith.net

- Each girl makes a flipchart or picture book of the Savior that she could look at during Sacrament Meeting.

- Have the girls make a Family Home Evening lesson with visual aids about the importance of the Sacrament and attending Church each week.

- Choose a special Sunday when all of the girls will sit together in Sacrament Meeting.

- Decorate a bulletin board together in the Primary room with pictures of each child in the Primary so they really feel like they belong there.

Other requirements

Write your testimony.

- Play inspiring music while you allow time for the girls to write their testimonies on pages 14 and 15 in their books.

- Talk about what a testimony is and the proper way to share it during Testimony Meeting at Church.

- Show the girls how to prepare a Book of Mormon to give to an investigator by marking key scriptures and writing their testimony in the front. Present the books to the missionaries to use for their investigators and/or challenge the girls to give them away to their friends.

- Teach the girls how to do calligraphy and write their testimonies on beautiful paper.

- Create a "Testimony Journal" that is passed around each month so that every girl gets an opportunity to write something down. When it is full it could be presented to the Bishop or Primary President.

- Before each girl spends time writing her testimony, have her create something fun to write with. Using floral tape, wrap the stem of a silk flower to a pen or pencil. Put beans in a clay pot or one that is decorated by each girl to hold her pen.

- Have the girls talk about how a testimony is like a balloon (it requires effort, it grows a little bit at a time, it can puncture easily, etc.) Have the girls pop balloons with a dart or by simply sitting on them. Inside each balloon they'll find slips of paper that reveal things they can do to gain a testimony such as praying, studying the scriptures, obeying the commandments, attending Church, etc.

- Share scriptures that teach about faith and how our testimonies can grow. Teach the girls about gardening and have each girl plant a seed. Have the girls write one sentence of their testimony each month and see how their testimonies grow to fill the page. Talk about the "roots" of a testimony and how we can "experiment upon the word." (Alma 32)

- Involve the girls in making a game board and cards that reveal things that either help or hinder our testimonies. Have them create their own marker and then play the game by taking turns selecting cards and moving ahead or behind spaces until they reach the end (a strong testimony).

- Teach the girls the Primary song "Testimony" and arrange for the girls to sing it in Primary or Sacrament Meeting.

- Do a sand art project and compare the grains of sand to the faith-promoting experiences that, added upon one another, create a beautiful testimony.

- Paint a wooden box that the girls can put their testimony-building items in: scriptures, journal, Faith in God booklet, handouts from Primary lessons, etc.

- Using building blocks, write a gospel principle on each one and have the girls take turns selecting a block to stack up and create a large structure. Be sure to include four blocks that say "Faith in Jesus Christ", "Repentance", "Baptism", and "The Gift of the Holy Ghost" to be the foundation of the building. Without even knowing it, they will be bearing their testimonies as they talk about the importance of each one!

- Show the girls how to create a "Why I believe" scrapbook journal, using photos, quotes, and written testimony.

- Create a Sacred Grove experience for the girls by taking a hike out in nature. Allow them to spend some quiet time alone with their scriptures and a journal. Invite a speaker to talk about the Book of Mormon and how he/she gained a testimony of it.

- Talk about how the Holy Ghost testifies and help the girls to recognize it, emphasizing that it can speak to us in different ways through our mind, heart, and spirit. Read scriptures that identify the fruits of the spirit.

- Teach the girls a new song about testimonies that is found at www.songsoftheheart.com/ltestimony.html

Memorize the Articles of Faith and explain what they mean.

- Teach the children different memorizing techniques to help them learn the Articles of Faith on page16 of their Faith in God booklets.

- Create a chart to keep track of which Articles of Faith all of the girls have passed off so that at a glance you'll know which ones to spend more time working on as a group. A good chart can be found at http://www.theideadoor.com/PDF%20Files/Primary/Articles%20of%20Faith%20Tracker.pdf

- Each girl earns a token each time she passes off an Article of Faith. The tokens can then be exchanged for utensils or toppings at a pizza or ice cream sundae party.

- Create a small poster or door hanger that could be displayed in each girl's bedroom where all of the Articles of Faith are displayed as a reminder for her.

- Have the girls create a "cheat sheet" for each Article of Faith by writing only the first letter of each word. Play games by mixing up the cheat sheets to see if they can guess the correct Article of Faith.

- Laminate the small Church cards that have the Articles of Faith on them to create bookmarks. Add a ribbon or beads to help mark the page.

- Play "Concentration" by having each girl draw a picture or two to go with another card that has the Article of Faith number or words written on it.

- Go to http://lds.about.com/od/wordsearchpuzzle/ for a word search puzzle for each Article of Faith.

- Have each girl choose an Article of Faith to write a poem about. Then take turns reading the poems and guessing which Article of Faith it applies to.

- Have each girl choose an Article of Faith to draw a picture clue about and then see if the others can guess which one it's about. Display the pictures each time you review the Articles of Faith with the girls.

- Play Pictionary to see if the girls can draw and guess visual clues about each Article of Faith.

- Have the girls make a mobile, writing each Article of Faith on a different element to be hung, such as on hearts or stars.

- While the girls practice reciting the various Articles of Faith have them make home-made ice cream. Check out the fun recipe for "Soup-Can Ice Cream in the July 1987 issue of *The Friend.*

- Present a charm to go on a key ring or bracelet for every Article of Faith memorized. Check out www.charmingldsgifts.com

- Do crossword puzzles that can be found online for each Article of Faith.

- Create a carnival atmosphere where the girls visit booths representing each Article of Faith to play games and win prizes each time they pass one off.

- Learn the Primary songs that go with each Article of Faith.

- Spray paint old keys gold and present one to each girl after she passes off an Article of Faith. By the time she graduates from Primary she should have earned the "Thirteen Keys to the Kingdom."

- Learn how to say one or more of the Articles of Faith in another language.

- Have a friendly competition with the Cub Scouts to see who can memorize all thirteen Articles of Faith first with the winners receiving a treat provided by the other group.

- Create a Jeopardy game, using words and clues from each of the Articles of Faith.

- Teach the contents of the Articles of Faith using an ABC game found at www.theideadoor.com

- Go online together to test the girls' knowledge on the Articles of Faith at http://lds.about.com/library/bl/primary/blarticlestest. htm

Complete activities in the guidebook for the four areas on pages 6-12.

- Use the ideas in the next few chapters to get your own creative juices flowing and have a brainstorm session with the girls for fun things they'd like to do that allow them to accomplish their goals.

- Create posters or decorative charts the girls could use to keep track of the progress on their goals if they'd like to use something in addition to the form on page 20 of their booklets.

- Put together a calendar with the girls on when they will pass off certain requirements, coordinating holidays and other events that fit nicely with the activities.

- Write all of the activity goals on slips of paper. Have the girls pick one out of hat each time you're together to decide which one you'll do next time.

- Play games with the other girls while each one has a turn to be interviewed and discuss her progress with a member of your Bishopric.

- Have an interview with a member of your Bishopric or Branch Presidency.

- Play games with the members of your Bishopric or Branch Presidency so the girls get to know them better and begin to fill comfortable with them.

- To help the girls better appreciate the leaders of their ward, decorate the outside of the ward clerks' office at Church with kind notes, photographs and drawings, thanking the Bishopric for their service to the ward.

- Prepare treats for the Bishopric to munch on during those long Sundays in December when they are busy doing Tithing Settlement.

- Invite the Bishopric to join the Primary during Sharing Time on Sunday and sing them some special songs you've been preparing for them.

- Create a gift to present to the Bishop on Father's Day for being such a good "Father" to the ward.

- Bake cookies and deliver them to the families of the Bishopric.

- Role-play an interview with the Bishop so the girls will know what to expect.

Chapter Six

Learning and Living the Gospel

- A fun gospel craft is to Mod Podge words on strips of paper to clear stones so the words show through. Word strips could include gospel principles, Articles of Faith, scriptures, "My Gospel Standards" or their names. You could even teach the girls to sew pretty velvet drawstring backs to keep their stones in or glue a magnet on the bottom so the stones could hang on their refrigerator at home.

- Sit on pillows, munching snacks while listening to a podcast of BYU devotionals, General Conference, or LDS music at www. apple.com/itunes.com

- Play "Stump The Bishop" (or whomever you want to stump). Have the girls bring miscellaneous items from home that are placed in a special box or bag. The "Stumpee" has to pull each item out and then explain how it relates to gospel principles. The girls could also do this with each other. You'll be impressed how creative they can be!

- Help the girls visit www.mormon.org to see all the great stuff that's there for them to learn about, as well as share with their non-member friends.

- Build gingerbread houses during the holiday season and talk about the gospel principles that we can build our lives and testimonies upon.

- Gather small items that are mentioned in the scriptures to create "I Spy" bags or bottles and share the stories about each object.

- Play "Ask the Scriptures." Girls write questions on slips of paper that are then put into a box and presented to the speaker who selects them one at a time and answers the questions. The girls could also take turns individually or as a group finding the answers. The girls will be more willing to ask real questions if they know their identity will be anonymous.

- Teach the girls how to make beanbags. Toss a beanbag to a girl, asking her a gospel-related question. When she answers the question, she tosses the beanbag to someone else and asks them a question.

- Before General Conference, help the girls learn more about the First Presidency and the Twelve Apostles. You can make game cards with their photos and bio and play "Go FISHers Of Men"! For game cards go to http://lds.about.com/library/bl/games/apostlecards2.pdf

- Have the girls sing Karaoke to Primary songs! Check out http://easy.karaokespace.info

- Teach the girls about food storage and sample different recipes using ingredients such as wheat, oats, and dried milk.

- Cut different lengths of pipe to create musical chimes. Learn how to play some Primary songs with them that could be performed in Sacrament Meeting or Sharing Time. You can find measurements and instructions online.

- Using masking tape, create a giant Tic Tac Toe board on the floor. The girls hold either a big, paper X or O to form teams. Ask scripture questions to review gospel principles and have a girl stand on the square of her choice after correctly answering the question.

- Using a big roll of paper, create a board game that teaches and tests the girls' gospel knowledge. They could create their own rules and design or tweak an already popular game like "Chutes and Ladders" or "Mormonopoly." Put pictures of the girls on "Activity Days Dollars."

- Have each girl choose several gospel terms and scramble the letters. The others try to guess what the word is and then everyone discusses it for a few minutes before moving on to another one.

- Set up a tour of your local Family Storehouse Center and teach the girls about self-reliance and the Church's welfare program.

- Play the CTR trivia game found at http://www.jennysmith.net/images/media/CTRTrivia.pdf

- Teach the girls how to make candles and talk about what it means to "wax strong" in the gospel. There are tons of recipes and techniques online.

- Tweak some of the popular TV game show ideas to help girls learn and review gospel principles. Shows that work well are Jeopardy, Password, Hollywood Squares, and Who Wants To Be A Millionaire. Play music from the show and make "Activity Days Dollars" to earn.

- Teach the girls how to make flannel board stories from the scriptures or Church history by gluing fabric to the back of pictures. The pictures can be given to your ward library or to be taken home and used for each girl's Family Home Evening.

- Invite each girl to bring a different kind of fruit. Teach them how to make smoothies and talk about the importance of good nutrition and the Word of Wisdom.

- A fun gospel "Cranium" game can be found at http://www.sugardoodle.net/Primary/Primary%20Cranium.pdf

- Play "Who Am I" by describing facts about a scripture person or quoting something they said.

- Put various items in a hat or bag and have the girls take turns finding scriptures that relate to that item.

- Check out http://abacuspc.hypermart.net/sem/ for some fun gospel-oriented board games.

- Teach the girls about emergency preparedness and help them create a 72-hour kit in a can, backpack, or bucket. There's even a clever idea for using an old sweatshirt online for a kit.

- Make paper dolls and design a modest wardrobe for them.

Chapter Seven

Serving Others

Some terrific resources where you can learn about service organizations and projects the girls could get involved with are: www.volunteermatch.org, www.serviceleader.org, www.volunteers.com and www.servenet.org

- Learn to crochet squares for the Red Cross "Warm Up America" Program. They collect squares from volunteers and then create blankets out of them for the needy. For information call (704) 824-7838 or go to www.warmupamerica.org

- Celebrate "Be An Angel" Day on August 22nd, do a service project, and make a cute angel craft. Fun ideas can be found at http://www.dltk-bible.com/paper-angels.html

- Hold a car wash but don't charge anyone money for the service. Give patrons a Pass Along card and let them know you were there to serve the community.

- Organize a book drive for your local Boys & Girls Clubs, hospitals, or shelters.

- Volunteer at the Salvation Army, Deseret Industries, or a local food bank.

- Girls love making crafts and they can do good works at the same time. Go to www.allcrafts4charity.org and www.bevscountrycottage.com to learn about projects they can make and donate.

- For outdoor service projects sponsored by the Keep America Beautiful Foundation, go to www.kab.org

- Teach the girls how to knit projects like clothes for stuffed bears that are given to children in crisis by Precious Pals or Project Linus. (www.projectlinus.org)

- Get the girls involved in collecting food that can be distributed locally through a food bank such as Second Harvest. (www.secondharvest.org)

- Collect toys for needy children before the holidays that can then be distributed through the Toys For Tots organization. (www.toysfortots.org)

- Find out how all of the Primary children in your ward and/or Stake can participate in National Youth Service Day or *USA Weekend's* Make A Difference Day.

- Wash windows on the cars parked at the temple and leave little notes that thank the patrons for their service. Be careful of car alarms!

- Make visual aids that could be given to the Primary teachers and Chorister, such as flannel board stories, music aids, object lessons, etc. Laminate the pictures so they will last a long time.

- Hold an "Unsung Hero" service project. Find out who in the ward has "quiet" callings such as a librarian, Church Magazine Rep, choristers, pianists, bulletin board person, Sunday program printer, etc. Invite them to a special dinner where you honor their efforts and let them know they are appreciated.

- Organize a Blood Drive by calling 1-800-GIVE-LIFE.

- Show support by attending community events. Involve your girls in volunteering and participating in them by making a float for a local parade, running in a 5K, passing out snacks at a craft fair, etc.

- Adopt a specific military Troop to pray for by signing up at http://www.presidentialprayerteam.net/manageadoptionslogin.php

- Sign up to be clowns in a local parade and pass out candy to the children.

- Pack up all of your stamping supplies and visit the children's trauma unit in your local hospital. Help the children decorate cards to give to their families, friends or even the hospital staff.

- Take any old cards you have received or made and cut the fronts off and send them to Sherrill Graff. She will add cardstock to them to make them a full card and add an envelope for each one. She and the Young Women in her ward will deliver them to their local Ronald McDonald house. They use them to thank volunteers and to cheer up sick children. The children's families can also send some out others, thanking them for their support and help in their time of need.

  Sherrill Graff
  605 Kendrick Place
  Boulder City, NV 89005

- Do something for the Cub Scouts or Boy Scouts to let them know you support the good works they are doing. See if you can help a Cub Scout with his goal to "do a good turn daily."

- Teach the girls how to make cinnamon rolls from scratch using different kinds of wheat (hard red, soft winter, etc.) Have them take home a batch for their families or make some for an early morning Seminary class.

- "Secret Grandmas." Get a list of all the older sisters in the ward and assign a few of the girls to each senior sister. Deliver secret gifts to them for a month. Bring them flowers, cards, goodies, and crafts. At the end of the month invite the senior sisters to a special presentation and reveal who their secret "grand-daughters" were.

- "Spa Night." Teach the girls how to do facials, manicures, pedicures, and hot oil treatments. Have them practice on each other so they can then go home and treat their mothers to a spa night.

- "Feed A Soul." or "We CAN Do It" Divide the girls into teams who will call ward members to let them know that next week the girls will be stopping by to pick up donated canned food items. Have a contest to see who can collect the most.

- Have sister missionaries speak about their choice to serve a full-time mission. Discuss how they prepared and the blessings that followed. Prepare some care packages that could be sent to the missionaries serving from your ward or branch.

- Many retirement homes have big BINGO events that the girls could help with. You could also sing for the residents, make and bring gifts for them, polish their fingernails, help them write letters to their families, and with permission, have the girls bring their pets for the residents to hold and play with.

- Stuff envelopes for a school, PTA, a charity, or some other non-profit organization.

- Have everyone bring non-perishable items to include in care packages for missionaries and military who are serving from your ward. Include uplifting letters.

- Make curtains for the ward's kitchen, nursery, Primary, the Young Women's room, Relief Society room, Bishop's office, or other classrooms.

- Make "Welcome To The Area!" packets for new move-ins. Include maps of the area, phone numbers, a ward directory, school and utility information, Parks & Recreation catalogs, etc.

- Make gifts the girls could give to military servicemen and women on Veteran's Day or Memorial Day such as a patriotic craft, plaque, cookies, an award, etc. Invite a Veteran to speak to the girls about his/her experience serving this country.

- Stencil dish towels that could be donated to the ward kitchen or bath towels that could be given as gifts at baptism. Tie them up with a ribbon and attach a note that says:
"May this ABSORB your troubles, BLOT out problems,
SOAK up sorrows, and WIPE away difficulties!"

- Using clean, dry soup cans or those big food storage cans, paint designs on the outside and fill with treats that can be given to others as gifts.

- Teach the girls how to give themselves manicures. Talk about all of the good service we can do with our hands and how we can place our lives in God's hands.

- Learn about famous Mormons at www.famousmormons.net and help the girls think about what good they contribute to the world.

- Arrange to visit an animal shelter to play with the animals and help clean up the stalls.

- Read children's stories into a tape recorder and package the books and tapes together as a set so they can be given to a hospital, Boys & Girls Club, library, preschool, school for the blind, or daycare center.

- Find out how your girls can participate in a Women's Walk for Breast Cancer, the March of Dimes, or some other local event to help fight terrible diseases.

- Talk to the Facilities and Public Works Department of your city to see what service projects your girls could do. They can usually think of ideas that would readily work such as painting over graffiti or cleaning up parks.

- Using the girls' handprints paint t-shirts, pots, aprons, binders, make Plaster of Paris designs, or other items. Talk about how we use our hands to bless others and how we can place our lives into the Lord's hands with our faith.

- Paint and wallpaper a shelter. Make curtains and other decorative items to make it feel like a home.

- Write to your local Congressman about issues that affect your community. Invite a local civic leader to speak about how they can contribute in a positive way. Write letters of appreciation to Congresswomen for setting such a great example of leadership.

- Teach the girls some sign language and check out the Church's web site about American Sign Language at www.asl.lds.org. See if there is a school for deaf children where the girls could practice their new skills and help out.

- Find out if there are some projects with Habitat for Humanity that your girls could help out with.

- Surprise everyone in your building by cleaning it! Tackle the kitchen and make labels for the cabinets, organizing their contents and cleaning the shelves. Reserve a cabinet or box for Lost and Find items.

- Have a progressive dinner, performing various acts of service in between courses.

- Teach the girls how to make a quilt that could be given to a shelter, high school seniors leaving for college, new babies in the ward, or someone in need.

- Go to the Bishop's Storehouse and can food for families in the ward who are unable to do the manual labor themselves. Check with your local cannery to find out about age restrictions on operating equipment. Most likely, they will not be able to use the equipment, but they could get a tour of the facility and prepare boxes and label cans for patrons.

- Invite a representative from the Red Cross to teach the girls about disaster relief, preparedness, and how the girls can help in their community.

- Do something nice for the Bishopric and/or presidencies of each auxiliary in your ward to let them know their hard work is appreciated.

- After learning how to do manicures, go to a retirement center and offer to give the ladies manicures and hand massages.

- Help your ward's Activity Director prepare for the next party or event by making decorations, centerpieces, posters, etc.

- Create a "Taste the Sweetness of Service" jar by filling a specially decorated jar for the Bishop and putting a piece of candy in it for every act of service each Primary child gives.

- Make meals for a widow or sister on bed rest that she could freeze and use later. The Bishop may help with funds for that.

- Sing the 7 Dwarves song "Hi Ho" but have it stand for something new . . . Happiness Is Helping Others.

- "Land of Oz." Host a *Wizard of Oz*-themed event to talk about getting a heart, head and courage to do service.

- Sign up ward members who are widows, elderly or home-bound to join the "Letter A Month Club." Prepare sweet cards and letters that could then be mailed every week to uplift and inspire them.

- Put together "Finals Survival Kits" to send to college students from your ward. Include a bag of "brain candy" to help them get through those long study hours.

- Plan a special dance for the married couples in the ward in the style of a prom, complete with photos, dinner, and crowing of a King and Queen.

- Learn about literacy and the Church's emphasis on helping others to read. Offer to help students in a Boys & Girls Club, after-school facility or members of your own ward.

- Plan a special luncheon for the Primary teachers and presidency to thank them for all they do for the children.

- Crochet leper bandages, baby caps, infant layettes, as well as other products used by the Church's Humanitarian Department. For more information contact:

  Latter-day Saint Humanitarian Center
  1665 Bennett Road
  SLC, UT 84104
  Telephone: (801) 240-6060
  Hours 8:00 AM - 4:00 PM, Monday through Friday

- Call your local LDS Social Services office. They usually have all kinds of projects they need help with.

- Make newborn hats that can be donated to hospitals. You can even buy one of those round looms which makes the project go very quickly and easily!

- Learn about "Locks of Love" if you have girls with very long hair who are considering cutting it.

- Invite the girls to take their pets to a retirement home to visit with the residents.

- If you have artistic girls, take them to a retirement home or children's hospital and have them draw portraits of the residents. If they aren't very good at drawing you could take Poloroid pictures or even digital pictures that could be printed out and brought back on another day.

- Create a Family Service Coupon book that the girls can use at home.

- Have a "Random Acts of Kindness" contest and see which team can complete the most in an hour.
- Take cookies to widows on Valentine's Day or other holidays.
- Plan a dinner for all of the Seminary teachers and their spouses so they can eat together before the annual CES "Meet A General Authority" broadcast in the winter.
- Decorate lunch bags for missionaries and fill them with yummy food and snacks for them to enjoy at a Zone conference.
- Help an older person write his/her autobiography. Record a video of them being interviewed, organize their photos, etc.
- Make hospital gift tray items such as nice poems rolled up with a ribbon and piece of candy.
- Make gift baskets to give to military wives for Mother's Day, Easter and/or Christmas.
- Find out how your girls and ward can help with Special Olympics.
- Paint and wallpaper a shelter or Boys/Girls Club.
- Build a Pinewood Derby track for your Cub Scouts if your ward or Stake doesn't have one.
- Build toy boxes or shelves for your building's nursery and/or Primary room.
- For tons more ideas check out http://www.theideadoor.com/LDS%20Service%20Projects.htm
- Find out if there is an "Operation Sack Lunch" program in your area where the girls could help prepare and pass out lunches to the homeless in a safe facility.

Chapter Eight

Developing Talents

- Create your own "Homemaking Olympics." Have fun and silly competitions that test such skills as sewing a button, reading a story, making a sandwich, ironing a shirt, making a bed, and braiding hair. Include an Opening Ceremony with flags the girls design, entertainment, and the Olympic theme song.

- Hold a video scavenger hunt and teach the girls how to properly use the equipment. Give them a list of items to find and film in the Church building or in your neighborhood if you are holding your activity at home.

- Teach the girls what a melodrama is and then have them create one! Perform live or record their show on video. The cornier the better! Use this year's Primary theme, a scripture, Primary song, or make-up a line or props they have to include in their play.

- Teach the girls how to make different kinds of pizza: deep dish, vegetarian, fruit, dessert, thin crust, meat lovers, etc. Learn how to make different kinds of crust too: Boboli, hand-made, Bisquick, deep-dish, thin, cookie, etc.

- Enter a local flower show, craft fair or 4-H event.

- Have a "HandyWoman" class where you teach the girls how to fix a squeaky door and repair other household items.

- Teach the girls how to make cinnamon rolls from scratch using different kinds of wheat (hard red, soft winter, etc.) Have them take home a batch for their families or make some for a Seminary class.

- Start a book club, or show the girls how to start one in their community, by choosing good books and creating a list of discussion items that could be included in a group setting.

- Take the girls to their local library and help them open an account and get a card if they don't have one already. Talk about the importance of reading good books throughout our lives.

- Invite speakers from the local hospital to teach babysitter-certification classes to your girls.

- Teach the girls "Powder Puff Mechanics" and how to do basic car maintenance.

- Learn how to make jewelry and/or care for jewelry properly.

- Learn how to make piñatas or other paper mache items. Talk about what we can learn from other cultures and their traditions.

- Teach the girls how to cook something and then give them a recipe they can add to their growing collection. Have the girls decorate a cute recipe book or folder, creating dividers based on categories the girls want to learn about such as: breads, things to do with pumpkins (after the fall holidays), desserts, chicken dishes, appetizers, fun drinks, etc.

- Invite your Ward Emergency Preparedness Specialist to teach a lesson on how to be better prepared for emergencies. Have the girls put together an emergency car kit, first aid kit or something they could add to their family's 72-hour home kit.

- Invite speakers from your local "ToastMasters Club" or high school Speech & Debate team to teach the girls how to prepare an effective Primary talk.

- Learn how to do outdoor cooking such as Dutch Oven cooking or BBQ. Have a contest with the Cub Scouts to see who can cook the best main course or dessert.

- Invite your stake webmaster to talk about the resources available on the Church's web site and how to use them. Find out if your ward has its own web site and see what's on it.

- Have goofy Olympic contests to get the girls excited about the upcoming Olympics. Learn about the host country.

- Teach the girls how to sew. Have them make bean bags for games in the Primary or, if their skills are more advanced, teach them to sew modest clothing.

- Learn how to bake bread. Contact your ward's Aaronic Priesthood leaders and let them know your girls will provide two loaves for next Sunday's Sacrament Meeting.

- Learn about reflexology and how to do pedicures. Talk about standing in holy places, "how beautiful are the feet of them that preach the gospel of peace" and discuss what we can learn from when the Savior washed the disciples' feet.

- Teach the girls how to cut different kinds of fruit. Make a fruit salad, ambrosia, or have a taster's table. Discuss all of the scriptures that talk about different kinds of fruit. Discuss the idea "By their fruits ye shall know them."

- Teach the girls to be smart . . . street smart . . . and protect themselves. Introduce them to some of the following web sites:

  www.vcpionline.org/mousetrap/index.html

  www.netsmartz.org

  www.missingkids.com

  www.familywatchdog.us/

- If your Primary doesn't have those cute fabric covers that identify each Primary class on the back of the chairs, teach your girls how to sew them and present them to your Primary during Sharing Time.

- Learn about other countries. Invite returned missionaries to give mini-lessons on the country where they served.

  Create a travel box where the girls can store special vacation photos and souvineers by decoupaging maps, postcards and other travel memorabilia.

- Have a talent show and invite the girls' families to be the audience.

- Teach the girls magic tricks they can use at how to wow their families during Family Home Evening.

- Teach the girls some sign language and check out the Church's web site about American Sign Language at www.asl.lds.org

- Learn how to take good pictures. If you live near a temple you could use that for a background and teach them about composition, light, etc.

- Invite the Mayor or City Council member to teach the girls how your local government works. Attend a City Council meeting or visit City Hall and meet the people who work there.

- Invite girls who are in middle school to sit as a panel of speakers and answer questions about their school, plugging the importance of education and good friends.

- Invite someone from a local bicycle store to teach the girls how to choose the right bike and take care of it. Go on a bike ride together. Find out if there is an amateur racing team in your town who could also come talk to the girls about what they do.

- "Scripture Clues At The Mall" Help the girls think harder about the scriptures in a fun way. Divide the girls into small teams and provide each group a set of scriptures and scripture reference clues that will direct them to various stores in the mall. Meet at the food court for refreshments.

- Teach the girls how to snorkel by practicing in someone's pool. Place items at the bottom that they have to dive and retrieve. Include lifesaving skills and water safety instruction.

- Teach the girls different styles of dance: western line-dance, hip hop, ballroom, salsa, etc. Choreograph a fun routine that could be performed at a quarterly Primary Activity or in a Road Show. Make a cute music video to a Primary song or by an LDS artist.

- Learn what it takes to put a play or concert together by attending a dress rehearsal of a local show. You'll be able to get in for free or else at a greatly reduced price and probably be able to meet the performers afterward.

- Read or act out the parable of the Talents and talk about how we can apply the lessons learned from it to developing our own talents. Encourage the girls to identify their unique talents as well as list the ones they'd like to develop.

- Learn about some of the unusual sports in the Olympics such as curling or rugby.

- Spend time in a pool doing water aerobics, snorkeling, playing pool-games, and learning life-saving techniques.
- Invite a hair stylist to demonstrate different things the girls can do with their hair, such as updos, French braids, twists, buns, etc.

Chapter Nine

Preparing For Young Women

Most girls are thrilled to be graduating from Primary and yet a bit apprehensive about joining the older teenage girls. There are big differences between the needs, interests, and maturity levels of an 11-year-old girl and a young woman of 17!

- Plan a "Bee All That You Can Bee" event where the Beehives can show them how much they can learn and grow during their years in the Young Women's program.

- Teach her some camp songs before camp so she'll feel comfortable joining in on the fun once she gets there.

- Help her memorize the Young Women theme so she doesn't feel awkward on Sunday when all of the other girls are saying it aloud together during Opening Exercises.

- Give her a "Young Woman Survival Kit." Cute suggestions can be found at www.christysclipart.com/survival.html

- Create a "Welcome" packet that includes all of the Young Women materials and welcome letters from all of the other girls.

- Assign a "Big Sister" from one of the Young Women to make sure she has someone to sit next to during Opening Exercises, knows about the activities, gets some fun treats or surprises in her mailbox, teaches her about the programs, and introduces her to the other girls.

- Coordinate a visit between a Young Women leader and the parents of the soon-to-be Beehive to explain all the ins and outs of the Young Women's program. For a first-time Beehive parent it can be overwhelming!

- Invite all of the young women and their leaders to go into the Primary room with balloons or flowers to escort the new Beehive to the Young Women's room on her first day.

- Invite the young women to a "Get To Know" you activity so they can get to know the girls better.

- Invite the Young Women presidency to speak about how their organization works. You could have a panel atmosphere so that the girls could ask them questions about the similarities and differences of the two organizations.

- Invite the Young Women to compete against the Primary in various contests such as daily scripture reading, memorizing scriptures, church attendance or whatever.

- Take the eleven year old girls on a "field trip" to attend Young Women's one Sunday. The next week talk about the similarities and differences. Ask the girls what they think they could learn and contribute to the Young Women's group.

- Create a "Meet and Greet." Attend Opening Exercises in Young Women's. Have the young women stand and recite their theme and then have the Primary girls recite "My Baptismal Covenant" on pages 2-3 in their booklet, "I Am A Child of God" on the inside of the front cover or "My Gospel Standards" on the back cover.

- Point out to the girls what talents and gifts she could offer to the Young Women so she feels valued and needed.

- "Sister To Sister" Have both the eleven year old girls and the Young Women draw names of someone in the other organization to bring surprises and treats to her secret sister for a month. Hold a special event where they can reveal their identities and enjoy their new friendships. Have the girls give the young women a flower with a note attached that says "Sister to Sister – Heart to Heart. You were my friend right from the start."

- Take turns reading aloud the article called "Welcome to Young Women" in the July 2006 issue of *The Friend*.

- Invite the Beehives in your ward's Young Women program to bake and decorate sugar cookies with your girls for an upcoming holiday. While they work, have the Beehives talk about all of the fun activities the Primary girls have to look forward to.

Graduating Girls

As the girls graduate from Primary, there are some special things you can do for them to let them know they will be missed and forever loved:

- Present her with a pearl bracelet or necklace and tell her that she is a Pearl of Great Price!

- Present her with an oil lamp or pretty light to let her know that you appreciate how she has been a shining example for all the other girls.

- Have a "Graduating Girls" event where you spotlight each girl and her accomplishments.

- Invite all of the other girls to write a letter of appreciation for the graduating girl and put them in a specially-decorated binder with photos of everyone.

- Hang pictures of all the graduating girls on a Primary bulletin board with information about their accomplishments.

- Give her a picture of your nearest temple and a basket with some things she'll need now that she gets to do baptisms at the temple, such as a white hair scrunchie, comb, picture of Christ, journal, a book about the temple, etc.

- Make a "spiritual survival kit" that includes a bookmark, a journal, a list of favorite scriptures that all of the other girls have written down, an uplifting book about prayer, etc.

- Invite the Primary presidency to join you and the graduating girls to a special lunch or dinner.

- Present her with a photo album of all the pictures you've taken of her during her Primary years. That's a hint for you to remember to take lots of pictures!

Chapter Ten

Motivation and Recognition

Help the girls understand that the suggested tasks in their book are not "busy work" but actually introduce the girls to things they will be doing the rest of their lives: studying the scriptures, setting goals, learning, growing, serving.

Every girl is unique and progressing at a different rate, so it's important for her to understand that the goals she selects are for her to improve herself and not to compete with others. Familiarize parents with the program and offer suggestions for them to support their daughter. Help the girls and their parents look at the activities they are already involved in and see how they could apply towards meeting some of the goals.

Once all of the requirements have been met, the Primary President and Bishop (or Branch President) sign the certificate and recognize the child's accomplishments in Primary.

- Have a plaque made that can be hung on the wall by the Bishop's office or in the Primary room for all to see the names of the girls who have received their Faith In God award.

- Create a lovely chart the girls can keep at home or use at church that will keep them motivated each week. Encourage positive reinforcement rather than negative competition.

- Plan at least two times during the year when the children can share what they have learned and accomplished with one another.

- Present a larger version of the certificate in the back of the book for them to frame and hang on their walls. A good one can be found at http://www.theideadoor.com/PDF%20Files/Primary/Faith%20in%20God/FIGfor%20girlscert.pdf

- There are several great ideas to help you keep track of all of your girls and their progress at http://www.ldsactivitydays.com/RecordKeeping.html

- Have the girls bring blankets, pillows, and their Faith in God books. Make pop corn and have the girls watch the video "Wives and Daughters of the First Presidency" while the leaders pull one girl out at a time to update her Faith in God book and go over her goals.

- Make sure her accomplishments are announced in Primary so all of the other children can applaud and be impressed.

- Have a monthly or quarterly P.I.E. night. "Personal Interviews Event" where each girl sits down with a leader and goes over her goals. While the other girls are waiting for their turn they can bake pies, eat or even work on a group project.

- Help the girl to focus on "What do I want to become?" not "What do I want to do?"

- Create a special binder for each girl to either keep at church or take home. Things you could include are a copy of the Faith in God booklet, a copy of "The Living Christ" and "The Family: A Proclamation to the World", a class list with phone numbers for the girls and the leaders, a monthly calendar, and notepaper.

- Each time a girl completes a goal she could earn a ticket to redeem for a topping on an ice cream sundae made at a special activity day in the future.

- Include a Faith in God article in your ward or Primary newsletter to spotlight some of the girls' accomplishments.

- Have a "You CAN do it!" can where the girls can select treats from each week when they pass off goals.

- Each girl can make a doll (wood, porcelain, fabric) and receive other elements for it each time she completes a goal. Items could be clothing, hair, jewelry, shoes, miniature cell phone, etc.

- Have each girl make a Noah's ark craft and receives an animal each time she completes a goal.
- Give each girl a charm bracelet or a necklace chain when she turns eight. Each time she completes a goal she earns a charm to add to her jewelry. Check out www.charmedmoments.com
- Each time a girl completes a task she earns a square of fabric that will become her very own quilt. Have a big quilt-making party at the end of the year.
- Buy an oil lamp and have the girls drop some "oil" into the lamp each week if they have completed a project or even worked on one. Talk about the Parable of the Ten Virgins and their own spiritual preparation. The girls could each have their own lamp or you could have one large one for all of the girls combined. Once the lamp is full you could choose to have a party or some other special reward.
- Create a poster with the girls' names posted, placing a sticker next to every girl who passes off a task each week. Once she has earned 5 stickers she gets a special treat.
- Present each girl with one piece of a Nativity set when she has finished each goal or at the end of each year's accomplishments. The completed set is something that will be cherished in her home now and when she has her own family.
- Present the girl with a picture of her shaking hands with the Stake President and/or Bishop and/or Primary President (or all of the above!) when she has completed all of the Faith in God goals.
- Add a pearl, bead or charm to a bracelet that is being created for every accomplishment the girl passes off. Have a jewelry making activity for all of the girls to get excited about it.
- Make a Faith in God Family Home Evening lesson to help family members understand the program and how they can support the Primary children in their family. Choose goals they can work on together.
- Have the girls decorate a Primary bulletin board with Faith in God information.

- Encourage the Primary Presidency to ask children to give talks on the Faith in God program and goals often during Opening or Closing Exercises on Sundays.

- Provide a "You Nailed It" basket the girls can pick from when they finish a goal. The basket will include a variety of nail polish, glitter, stick-ons, Emory boards and other nail care items.

- Give the girls a cute little reminder each month to work on their goals such as a piece of gum with a note that says "Stick To Your Goals."

- Have a weekly Spotlight moment each time you meet by shining a flashlight on each girl while she talks about her accomplishments.

- Find a nice receptacle to put candy in as the girls complete their assignments. When the jar is full, present it to the Bishop to put on his desk in his office for him to share with future visitors.

- Show the girls that it's easy to get a good "jump start" on their goals by doing one all together the first week of the month. Play jump rope, learn about jumping beans, and have the girls do a few jumping jacks before they get refreshments.

- Encourage the leaders to work towards earning their Faith in God award and let the girls know it. They will be impressed and motivated by their leaders' examples. Have a healthy competition between the girls and the leaders to see who can pass off the most goals within a certain time period. Whichever group "wins" is treated to a special treat or event by the other group.

- Begin a "Pie Plunge" tradition. For every goal passed off within a certain time frame the girl gets to throw a pie at the Bishopric or Primary leaders at a "Pie Plunge" activity day. Cut holes in big sheets of plastic for the leaders to put their heads through. Thrown pies could just be whipped cream on pie plates. Save the real pie for dessert!

- Write Faith in God goals on slips of paper and have the girls draw one out of a hat to decide which one they're going to do that day or, to allow more preparation time, for next time.

- When the girls finish a goal they get to put their name in a jar. Once a month or quarter, draw a few names of winners to receive a special treat.

- If you want to create a progress chart to display on the wall for everyone to see, then have each girl make-up an alias name so that the girls won't be embarrassed.

- Have the girls make magnet reminders to put on their mirrors or refrigerators at home to remind them to work on their goals.

Chapter Eleven

Parental Support

Parents have the responsibility to help their children learn and live the gospel. Primary leaders and teachers ASSIST parents in this great responsibility. Help parents understand that your role is to help them. If parents and leaders work together as a team the children will be surrounded by love, support, guidance, and protection.

Getting support from the parents of the Primary girls is extremely important for the progress and success of your program. When the parents see that their daughter is being blessed by her attendance they will be more eager to make sure she goes to Church and Activity Days. Parents will become very supportive when they see your activities and efforts are helping their daughter to strengthen their home and family!

LDS families have very busy lives and, most likely, the parents are trying to coordinate the activities of several children at the same time. When you communicate with the parents and let them know ahead of time what you've planned for their daughter, they will be able to support your calendar with enthusiasm. Here are a few ideas to help get more support from the parents:

- Make sure they have a copy of the Faith In God booklet.
- Invite parents to join you every now and then for activities and you just might be able to pass off the requirement on page 9 of the Faith in God booklet!
- Send them weekly e-mails with an updated calendar.
- E-mail them pictures that were taken from last week's activity.
- Send them a monthly newsletter.

- Find out what their talents are and recruit them to teach classes or activities where they can share their skills.
- Do in-home visits with their daughter and include them.
- Invite them to hold a special activity in their home.
- Invite them to attend a special day and time when parents of all the Primary children will be in the temple, praying for their children.
- Honor them at a special Parents Appreciation activity.
- Encourage their daughters to write them thank you letters.
- Provide opportunities when the girls can make special crafts and gifts for their parents.
- Always speak positively about the parents in front of the girls so they will see that you respect them.
- Invite the parents to take turns bringing refreshments for special occasions and to be involved in the events.
- Write them a thank you letter, expressing how much you appreciate all of the good things that they have taught her.
- Call them up and ask them what they think you could do to better touch their daughter's heart and help her want to live the gospel.
- Invite them to be guest speakers in a panel, addressing a topic of a particular goal.
- Write complimentary articles about each girl that could be submitted to your ward newsletter.
- Have a look-alike contest, showcasing photos of the girls and their parents when they were babies.
- Have a 50's, 60's, 70's or 80's night and invite the parents to come and share their experiences of being children and/or in the Primary. Help the girls appreciate their parents.
- Have a family tree climbing activity where the girls can bring photos, pedigree charts, and other memorabilia to share what they know about their ancestors. If you invite the parents they will be grateful for the opportunity to talk about the legacy their parents have left.

- Let parents know what goals you're emphasizing each month and include a list of things they could talk about and do with their daughter at home to reinforce what you are trying to accomplish.

- Involve the parents in a big craft project or something they can work on with their daughter.

- Have a Father/Daughter or Mother/Daughter cooking contest.

- Ask the parents how you can help them get their daughter to church and activities on time.

- Ask parents to keep you informed of their daughter's special events such as piano recitals, sports events, competitions, performances and other occasions you could attend to show you care.

- Visit her home and see her bedroom. Let her tell you about her favorite things in her room. Let her parents hear you expressing interest in what she does.

- Pray for the parents and let them know you are praying for their success in raising such a wonderful girl.

- Encourage the parents to write a "love letter" to their daughter for a special occasion.

- Send your daughter home with ideas for Family Home Evening lessons, refreshments, games and other activities for her family.

- Create a special scrapbook for each girl. Add photos of her and other momentos during her time in Primary. She can even work on it with you. Present it to the parents when she graduates or at the end of each year.

- Help each girl recognize the unique challenges her family faces and talk about how she can be a blessing to her parents and family.

- Have all of the children adopt one of the girl's families each month. The girls could write letters of appreciation, do a "heart attack", bring them goodies, give them an award, help baby-sit, help them with yard work, or invite them to be the guests of honor at a special evening.

- Have a cooking contest and then create a special Primary cookbook with all of the entries. Each girl can choose her mom or dad to help so it's a team effort and contest. You can even throw in a family history twist to it by requiring that all recipes must be either a family favorite or one that has been passed down in their family.

- Put ideas for creative, fun family activities onto colored slips of paper and then into a decorated mason jar or even one of those round, cardboard oatmeal boxes. Have every girl create one for her own family to use and talk about how the family who plays together stays together! Talk about other fun family traditions and ways to strengthen the family closeness and create special memories.

- Encourage your Bishopric to hold a special Parents Meeting on the 5th Sunday of each month, perhaps during the Sunday School hour or during a combined Relief Society/Priesthood lesson that focuses on the Primary and how parents can support them. Familiarize parents with the Faith in God goal programs so parents can ask their children informed questions at home and celebrate their progress.

- Have the girls decorate a mat that will go around a framed copy of "The Family: A Proclamation to the World."

- Encourage the girls to seek a Father's Blessing, perhaps at the beginning of each school year.

Fathers

As children develop close relationships with their fathers they will be able to better understand how much their Heavenly Father must love them. Be sensitive to the girls who don't have a father available to attend special events by inviting their Home Teacher, Bishop or even an older brother.

- Hold a Daddy/Daughter Nerds activity. Dress up like real goobers and play nerdy games. Make the invitations look like pocket protectors. Play games using calculators, math, trivia, duct tape, and broken glasses.

- Play dodgeball in the gym with the dads.

- Create a Daddy/Daughter Date. This could be a formal dinner and dance or a more casual western hoe down with Sloppy Joes. Create a fun evening where the girls can play with their dads and create special memories. Be sure to take one of those "prom-type" pictures of each girl with her father in front of a specially-decorated background. I still remember the dress I wore when I went with my own father to this kind of event!

- Spend some time talking about Heavenly Father and his divine attributes. Point out that a loving Heavenly Father gave us earthly fathers so we could learn more about what our father in heaven is like. Have the girls' fathers walk into the room carrying flowers for each girl. Invite each father to share what he has learned about Father in Heaven by becoming a father. Bring lots of tissue, as there will be tears shed!

- Begin a "Donuts & Dads" annual tradition. You guessed it . . . play games with donuts such as trying to eat a donut hanging from a string, Tic Tac Dough, donut hole rolling contest, Guess the Flavor contest, see how many donut holes the dads can get in their mouth at once, etc.

- Invite the brethren to a "Dads & Daughters in Dungarees" event. Have them perform a dirty service project such as pruning a widow's trees, painting a house, cleaning up a yard, etc.

- The fathers will appreciate the opportunity to spend time with "Daddy's little girl." Invite the dads to bring baby pictures of their daughters and tell all about their daughter's life growing up.

- Hold a "Dancing With Dads" event. Teach the dads and their daughters how to ballroom dance.

- Invite the men to "Dad's Duds." Help the girls to learn about boys' and men's fashion by doing a makeover with their dad.

- Design an activity using themes from the book "The Little Princess." Decorate with Indian décor and share tidbits from the book.

- Hold an annual "Sugar Daddy" contest. Have each Father/Daughter pair enter a dessert-making contest or see what they can construct using sugar cubes.

- Hold "Gym Night" or "Playground Pals." Play broom hockey, slide across the floor in socks, jump rope, and do some of the other games suggested in the game chapter.
- To get the fathers used to the idea that their little darling is going to want to borrow the keys some day, give each father/daughter a large appliance cardboard box that they have to transform into a car. Watch a movie together at the "drive in."
- Play flag football outside on the grass! Have each father and daughter make up a cheer.
- Have the girls sing some of the Father's Day songs in the Children's Songbook. Teach the fathers to sing this to the Primary tune of "Popcorn Popping."

> *I looked out the window and what did I see?*
> *My little girl changing right in front of me.*
> *Life has brought me such a big surprise.*
> *She is growing up right before my eyes.*
> *Wish I could take her and hold her tight.*
> *Keep her forever in my sight*
> *But it can't be so....It's just not the plan*
> *Someday she'll find her a special man.*

- Video tape sweet messages from the parents and play it for the girls.
- Design a Father/Daughter Newlywed game.
- Have a picnic and hoe-down outside.
- Design a "Turning Hearts To Fathers" activity. Have the fathers join their daughters in the Family History Center to see what information they can find together. Serve heart-shaped cookies for dessert.
- "Mission Impossible." Dress up like spies and solve mysteries together (like how to understand girls).
- Learn how to fix cars and do simple home maintenance together.
- Hold a "Daddy/Daughter Dinner Dance." Dress up very formally for a fancy dinner, dancing and etiquette night.

- Have a "Luau" and teach dads to do the hula and one of those stick dances!
- Play "Wheelbarrow Baseball." The girls hit the ball with a bat and then hop into a wheelbarrow to be pushed around the bases by their dads.
- Make a special gift for the mother.
- Here's a fun activity for Cinco de Mayo! Make piñatas together, eat Mexican food, learn a Mexican dance and some Spanish words. Find out how the Church is growing in South America and where the current temples are.
- Invite the girls' fathers to share "Missionary Moments." Encourage them to share experiences, photos, and food from their missions with the girls. Have each father/daughter pair do creative door approaches like they're missionaries.

Fun contests and races to play with dads:
- The dad has to braid his daughter's hair.
- The daughter has to shave her dad's face blindfolded. Use tongue depressors as the razor.
- The father and daughter have to run a distance with the daughter standing on his shoes.
- The father and daughter work together to solve a brain teaser.
- The dads stand behind a sheet with little holes cut out, sticking their noses through the holes. The girls have to "pick" which one belongs to their dad.
- The girls stand barefoot behind a divider (rolling chalkboard) and the dads have to find their daughter's feet.
- The girls have to correctly put a tie on their dad.
- Tape-record each father's voice and see if the girls can guess who they are.
- See who can snarf a plate of gelatin the fastest.
- "Guess Who?" Ask the dads ahead of time to tell you one crazy thing they had done when they were younger. Write them on slips of paper and read them one by one, having the girls vote on who they think it was.

- Play 'Whoops!' The fathers lay on their backs with an ice cream cone in their mouth (opening facing up). The girls stand on a chair over their respective father with a bowl of tapioca pudding or ice cream and a spoon. The race is to see who can fill the cone first. Then they switch (father on chair, daughter on floor) Hey, fair is fair!

- Shave a balloon. Put shaving cream on a blown-up balloon. Race to shave it first.

- Have a food relay by placing various edible items in each team's bag. One person races to the bag, eats the item and runs back to tag the next person on the team.

Mothers

As the Activity Day leader you want to be a positive role model for the girls, but you should be careful not to allow the girls to place you above their own mother in esteem, attention or time. Help forge the bond between mother and daughter. Create opportunities to support their relationship and create lasting memories for them together.

- Work with your Relief Society leaders to plan special events for mothers and their daughters at an Enrichment Night or other event.

- Plan a Mother/Daughter service project. Sew baby blankets for hospital, crochet newborn hats, bake cookies for widows, make curtains for the church building, etc.

- Play a Mother/Daughter Newlywed game to see how well they know each other.

- Hold a Fashion Follies show of either real fashion tips or goofy ones.

- Design a Mother/Daughter Tea Party (Herbal of course!) Decorate tables with rose petals and fine china. Serve crumpets, scones, tea sandwiches and learn about etiquette. Invite everyone to wear (and even make) fancy hats and white gloves.

- Host a "Garden Party" by decorating with an outdoor theme or actually holding a party outside! Play croquet, wear fancy hats, and speak with British accents.

- Create a spa experience. Learn how to make bath salts, bubble bath and bath bombs (tons of recipes online), do facials, pedicures, manicures, etc.
- Plan a "Mums The Word" activity where mothers and daughters learn how to arrange flowers together.
- Invite mothers to share photos and memories from their wedding day. Embroider handkerchiefs and serve wedding cake.
- Talk about a mother's touch. Learn how to give massages to each other.
- Send out invitations to a "Sugar and Spice and Everything Nice" event. Learn how to make fancy desserts such as swan cream puffs, éclairs, flambé, etc.
- Have a slumber party! Encourage everyone to wear modest pajamas and do "girl" things!
- Hold a "Joy Luck Club" activity where you serve Asian food, talk about the importance of girlfriends and celebrate sisterhood!
- Talk about the scripture that says a woman of virtue is more priceless than rubies and learn how to make different kinds of jewelry. Read stories out of the "Book of Virtues" by William J. Bennett.
- Plan an "Annie Get Your Gun" Western theme party. Learn how to cook various food items on a BBQ, have a squirt gun contest (aim at plastic items outside) and talk about strong women in history.
- Have a beach party indoors. Have a fashion show with modest bathing suits, talk about skincare, sunscreen, sit on beach chairs and learn how to make tropical drinks.
- Become "Scrapbook Queens." Learn new techniques for creating photo albums and beautiful scrapbooks.
- Invite the mothers to share their humorous and poignant motherhood experiences with the girls to help them know how to prepare for their own future families. You could even invite the Mother of the Year from your state to speak to everyone. Contact www.americanmothers.org
- Make potpourri or sachets.

- Create "stores" to look like a mall and "go shopping" together. Mother/Daughter pairs earn play money to spend by filling out a questionnaire of things they have accomplished that week (study the scriptures, Family Home Evening, laundry, dishes, homework, help someone, bake, etc). Learn exercise tips at the Sporting Goods store, buy a manicure at the Spa, attend a fashion show at the clothing boutique, and buy refreshments at the Food Court.

- Create a "Glamour Shots" experience for the girls and their mothers. Dress them up with fun accessories and take pictures of them separately and together. Show make-up and hair tips.

- Women and girls love candles. Teach them how to make different kinds, scent them, decorate with them and put small items inside the wax. Talk about what it means to wax strong in the gospel.

- Make or collect items for a Women's Shelter together. Talk about domestic violence and learn how to protect against it.

- Talk about all of the mothers in the scriptures and how we can be more like them.

- Have an "Extreme Makeover" activity. Invite the mothers to learn makeover tips with their daughters or have them dress and style each other.

- Talk about generations. Invite grandmothers, mothers, and daughters to share a special evening together, talking about the legacy women have in families.

- Hold a "Put Your Best Foot Forward" event where the moms and girls learn how to do pedicures, purchase the right kind of shoe, give foot massages, and model stylish footwear.

- Decorate frames and take pictures of the girls with their mothers.

- Teach the girls and their moms how to make chocolates or lollipops with candy molds. Make giant chocolate-covered Rice Krispy kisses.

- Make decorative soaps and talk about "Cleanliness is next to Godliness."

- Design a necklace hanger. Cut out a piece of cardboard into the shape of a heart and cover with batting and pretty fabric. Screw small hooks into the front.
- Make pretty paperweights.
- Make one of those photo holders out of twisted wire and secure onto a decorative weight made out of clay.
- Design heart-shaped brooches out of Plaster of Paris.
- Create a puzzle pin. Spray paint puzzle pieces red or pink and glue together in the shape of a heart. Glue a pin on the back.
- Make flower coasters, coffee table decorations or paperweights by arranging flowers in between two small pieces of glass. Wrap metallic tape (slide masking tape) around the edges.
- Enter "Mother's Day Poem" on any search engine and you'll find a million to choose from to attach to the gift. Here are some web sites for a few more craft gift ideas:
  www.enchantedlearning.com/crafts/mothersday/
  www.dltk-kids.com/crafts/mom
  www.theholidayspot.com/mothersday
  www.daniellesplace.com/html/mothersday.html
  www.kidsdomain.com/craft/_gifts.html
  www.familycrafts.about.com/od/mothersday/
  www.123child.com/easter/mother.html
  www.theideadoor.com/MotherDay.html
  www.garvick.com/annual/mothers_day/crafts.html
  www.homeandfamilynetwork.com/holidays/mothers.html

Chapter Twelve

Get to Know You
Fun and Games

Before we can serve the girls under our care we need to know them and understand their unique needs. Sometimes young girls can be shy. Sometimes they need a little gentle prodding to open up. Sometimes wards get divided and you need to provide opportunities for the girls to feel more united. Sometimes girls just wanna have fun! For all those reasons and more, here are a few fun ideas to put some spark into your Activity Days. Think of them as just a brainstorm to get your own creative juices flowing. Ask the girls to think of a gospel application to your game or activity and you'll be impressed with their creative answers!

Activities

- Take pictures of each girl standing like a paper doll. Have the girls cut the legs, arms, and head off each picture and then mix them up to create "new" girls. Show the girls how to appreciate the similarities and differences of their group.

- Have a "Brown Bag It" activity. Give each girl a brown paper bag to take home and fill with things that describe her personality and life. Everyone returns the next time you gather with their brown bags and shares what is in them. Have a brown bag dinner. Give the girls a small item in another brown bag to take home that will remind them of what they have in common with all the other girls in the Primary program.

- We'll call this activity "Flower of Friendship." Each girl brings a flower that best represents her and explains why she chose that one. Create a bouquet and talk about what flowers need to grow, comparing your class to a blossoming flower. Have the girls make tissue paper flowers or learn how to arrange flowers as an activity.

- Teach the girls the "ABC's of Friendship." Invite the girls to create a list of friendship rules from A to Z. Create a contract they can sign that encourages them to be their best and create a loving class environment for others.

- Have the older Primary girls each adopt a "Little Sister" from the younger ones. The identity of the "Big Sister" can either be a secret while she does nice things anonymously or else everyone can know everyone else's identity and they do things together during special combined activities, as well as sitting together on Sundays.

- Begin a "Friendship Basket." There are several variations to this. One girl fills a basket with things that tell about herself. She talks about why she chose those items and then she picks a slip of paper out of a jar to read the name of the next girl who will get a turn to do the same thing. She can present her items as gifts to the next girl. To prevent competition and overspending, another variation is for her to simply do a "show and tell" and take the items back home.

- Create a "Binder That Binds." After each meeting a girl is chosen to take home a binder that has been filled with a questionnaire or simply blank pages. The girl answers the questions and/or decorates a blank page to tell about herself. She shares the information and then passes it on to the next girl to take home the subsequent week.

- Teach the girls about "Friendship Knots." Make pretzels or homemade bread knots and talk about the qualities of a true friend: Knot critical, Knot thoughtless, Knot judgmental or irresponsible. A true friend is Knot to be taken for granted, knot to be forgotten, knot just a blessing but a miracle. Let's Knot let it slip away!

- Have each girl make a collage poster of things that describe her. The girls can try to guess who made each poster or they could simply take turns telling the others about why she created hers the way she did.

- Have an annual cake decorating contest. Give small groups an unfrosted, single layered cake (or cupcake) and a bowl of frosting. Place small bowls filled with candies, fruits, candy sprinkles, chocolate chips, coconut, raisins, nuts, etc. in the center of the table. Set a time limit for decorating. Have pre-appointed judges award prizes when the decorating is completed. Award prizes for the most original, most creative, etc. making sure each cake is awarded a prize. Gee, guess what's for dessert?

- While singing Primary songs pass around a bag of "Friendship Fudge". The girls mix the following ingredients together in a gallon ziplock baggie by gently squeezing the bag when it comes to them. Talk about how the rewards are sweet when we work together.

> 4 cups powdered sugar
> 3 ounces softened cream cheese
> ½ cup softened margarine
> ½ cup cocoa
> 1 tsp. vanilla
> ½ chopped nuts

* Vickie Hacking created a wonderfully comprehensive questionnaire for Young Women leaders to give to their girls, which could also be effectively used in Primary. It's a great starting place to learn more about each of the girls you have a stewardship over and is entitled "All About Me." It can be found at: www.lds-yw.com/html/yw_files.html (Look under the section "Leader Help.")

* Play "Truth or Dare." Have girls pull leader-approved questions out of a hat that they have to answer or else choose a "dare" card out of another hat. Make sure the questions and the dares will not offend or embarrass anyone but rather endear them to each other.

- Do the "Each One of Us is Unique" activity from the book *The Crayon Box That Talked* by Shane DeRolf. Present each girl with a box of crayons and celebrate the differences in one another.

* Begin "Amish Friendship Bread" by creating a starter dough that is then passed on to another and then another. By the time the dough has been shared by all of the girls have a bread-making activity.

Games

- Play water baseball by adding wet elements such as a kiddie wading pool filled with water for first base, a block of ice the girls have to sit on for second base, a bucket of water the player has to stick her foot in at third base, and a long length of visqueen or plastic between third base and home plate that the girls have to slide on. Keep a hose nearby to keep the plastic wet and give players in the field squirt guns or water balloons to use on players racing by them.

- "Birthday Line" Take some tape and make two parallel lines on the floor about a foot wide. Everyone has to stand in a row inside the lines and make sure their feet aren't touching the tape lines. They can stand side by side in the line so that the task is not impossible. Now tell them that they have to arrange each other in birthday order without stepping out of or on the lines. As people step out of the line, they're eliminated and the amount of space you have to move around increases so it gets easier.

- "Squeeze!" This game encourages creative thinking. Get 4 long pieces of string to form a square on the floor. The object is to fit the entire group into increasingly small spaces. Once the group can fit into a square of one size, make the square smaller each time. Have a competition between the girls and the leaders to see who is more creative. Talk about how it's cool to be "square" by living the standards of the church. Have the girls decorate blocks of wood by adding faces and hair so they "wood" remember to have Faith In God.

- "People Bingo." Make a Bingo grid with a "FREE" space in the center. In all of the other spaces, write things such as "Has been to Utah", "Has completed a Faith in God goal, "Has seen the movie Napoleon Dynamite", "Born in another state", "Has pierced ears", etc. The girls have to walk around the room and get the signature of a person who meets the criteria for each section. Depending on how many people are playing the game, you might want to implement a rule that a person can only sign another player's paper in two spots. The first person with a completed card wins!

- What's In A Name?" Participants stand in a circle, arms distance apart. Ask each person to think of a verb and action which starts with the same letter as the person's first name ("Jumping Janice" or "Kickboxing Kelly" for example.) The person does the action and yells out their action-name, then points to someone else. Try to go faster and faster until everyone knows everyone's name or is laughing to hard to play any longer, whichever comes first.

- "The Thing About String." Without telling anyone what the game is have each girl cut a piece of string or yarn from a roll. Tell them to make it as long or short as they wish. Now explain that the game is to have each girl take a turn and talk about themselves for as long as it takes them to wrap the string around their finger. Another variation is to assign each girl a cut piece of string that has a match that was given to someone else in the room. They have to find their match, sit together and then talk until they are finished wrapping the piece around one finger.

- "M&M's." Get a bag of M & M's and some small cups (like Dixie cups). As each person comes in to the room, give them a cup with a few candies and ask them not to eat any yet. After everyone has been seated in a circle, tell them you are going to go around the circle and for every color of candy they have, they have to tell the group as many things about themselves as the color represents. You can make up whatever categories you would like. For example, BLUE=Family, RED=Pets, BROWN = talents, GREEN = goals, etc.

- "Time Flies!" Have everyone write down a topic on a separate piece of paper and then put the slips of paper in a bowl or hat. Don't tell any other players what it is. Possible suggestions: famous Americans, TV shows, artists, music styles, cartoons, etc. Each person takes a turn picking a slip of paper out of the hat and talking for exactly one minute. Set a timer. If that person pauses, changes the subject or says "um" or "uh" then another person takes her place, yelling out "Time flies!" If the person can speak for the entire minute she earns two points. If someone else is speaking when the timer runs out she receives one point. The person with the most points when all the topics are gone wins!

- "To Tell The Truth." Everyone thinks of two things about themselves that are true (I've skied on Lake Mead, I have eaten duck) and one thing that is not true but might sound reasonable. (I won a high-jump contest, I won a baby beauty contest, etc.) The group has to decide which of the three items are true and false.

- "Telling a Yarn." Have everyone stand in a circle fairly close together and toss a ball of yarn to each other. When you catch the yarn you have to tell something about yourself, such as a hobby or something that no one knows. You then hold on to a piece of the yarn and toss the ball to someone else. Keep tossing and talking until you form a giant spider web. Then get out a beach ball and put it on the web. Talk about how we need to be unified as a group to keep the ball on top of the string. Have someone use scissors to snip a few strings here and there, while giving examples of negative things we might say to one another. Eventually the ball will fall through the web. Emphasize how our actions and words affect the group as a whole.

- "Mine Field." Create a "mine field" in a room by distributing balls, cans, foam noodles, and other objects on the floor. Divide the group into pairs. The challenge is for one of the girls in each pair to verbally guide her blindfolded partner through the minefield. Switch so that each girl can do both parts. See which pair can get through the maze the fastest.

- "Three Things." Each girl pairs up with another girl. They have to find three things they have in common and then present their findings to the rest of the group.

- "It's In The Bag." Open a big, grocery-sized paper bag and place it in the middle of the floor. Each person takes turns picking it up, but you can only do it using one of these three methods:
    1. You must pick up the bag with your teeth
    2. You must stand on one leg only
    3. You must not touch your hands on the floor.

    In the first round everyone gets a turn. If someone breaks one of the rules, she is out of the game. Before each round cut off one or two inches from the bag. The last one who is able to pick up the bag wins!

- Teach the girls how to play BUNKO. It's a fast-moving game where the girls will mix up partners a lot.

- "You're All A Bunch of Animals!" Give each girl a slip of paper with the name of an animal on it. They must locate the other members of their animal group by imitating that animal's sound. No talking is allowed.

- "Cooperative Musical Chairs." This activity is a twist on the familiar musical chairs game. Set up a circle of chairs with one less chair than the number of participants. Play music as everyone walks around the chairs. When the music stops, everyone must sit in a seat. Unlike the traditional game, the person without a seat is not out. Instead, someone must make room for that person. Then remove another seat and start the music again. The girls end up on one another's laps and sharing chairs! Afterward, stress the teamwork and cooperation the game took, and how the girls need to accept one another to be successful.

- "Evolution." Everyone begins as an 'egg,' so people have to pretend to be an egg. Find another egg and play 'rock, paper, scissors' with the other egg. Whoever wins gets to 'evolve' into a chicken, so now the chickens have to pretend to be chickens. Whoever loses remains an egg. Then the chickens must find other chickens in order to play rock, paper, scissors. The eggs must play with other eggs. Whoever wins evolves. Whoever loses de-volves. The loser between two chickens will become an egg again. The winner will become a dinosaur and pretend to be that. Loser eggs remain eggs. Again, like animals play rock, paper, scissors with like animals. Losers de-volve into what they were previously. Winners between two dinosaurs evolve into the highest form of evolution: either ELVIS or the ENLIGHTENED ONE, in which case they would pretend to be ELVIS or sit down and say OM, depending on how you choose to play the game.

- "Over The Wall." Divide the group into two teams. Two members of the team hold a rope about three to four feet above off the ground. The object of the game is to get everyone over the rope. No one can go under the rope. Before you start transferring people over the 'wall,' you meet as a team and decide how to get everyone over. Time the teams. If you don't have a large enough group, you can do this as one group.

- "Tower of Babel." Give each team the same materials: paper cups, empty cans, paper, balls, etc - anything you can think of. Using all the materials (points deducted for each object not used) the object is for each team to build the tallest freestanding tower without talking!

- "Building Bridges." Using mini marshmallows and toothpicks, each team has to build a bridge. Set your criteria - longest bridge (that doesn't break in the middle); tallest bridge (inches from the ground); bridge that can support the most weight, most creative design, etc.

- "Fruit Basket." Put out enough chairs for everyone minus one. Everyone playing needs to be given the name of a fruit (apple, orange, banana, etc.) The person without a chair yells out the name of one of the fruits. Each person who has been named that fruit then has to get up and move to another chair while the person in the middle tries to steal one of the seats. The person without a seat now becomes the caller. The caller can yell out two or more fruits at a time. If she yells "Fruit Basket" then everyone has to get up and move. The game continues until everyone has had a chance to be the caller. A way to learn more about the players is instead of calling out fruits, the person in the middle calls out something about herself or something she has done ("everyone who's been to Hawaii" or everyone who's had braces) and they change places quickly, leaving another person in the middle. Make sure that they go beyond saying things like, "everyone who is wearing blue" or other simple and mundane things. It has to be something that is special about them, playing a particular instrument or knowing how to ride a horse, etc. Emphasize the fact that you want to get to know something about them you may not have known before.

- "Balloons." Choose three different colors of balloons to represent the Primary age groups. Blow them up and scatter them all over the room on the floor, including under chairs and tables. The girls are not allowed to touch the balloons with their hands, but by only using their feet they have to gather their colored balloons to a certain corner of the room without being stolen by the other groups. The winning team is the group who can gather all of their balloons first. Another element of the game is to put slips of paper inside the balloons and when the teams have gathered their balloons they can then pop the balloons to read assignments, solve a riddle or whatever task you want them to perform to determine the real winner.

- "Quite A Pair." Provide each girl with two index cards. Ask each girl to write a brief description of her physical characteristics on one index card and her name on the other. Put all the physical characteristic index cards in a shoe box, mix them up, and distribute one card to each girl, making sure that no one gets her own card. Give the girls a few minutes to search for the person who fits the description on the card they hold. There is no talking during this activity, but they can walk around the room. At the end of the activity, tell the girls to write on the card the name of the young woman or leader who best matches the description. Then have everyone share their results. How many guessed correctly?

- "People in a Pot." Divide the group into two teams. Write down the names of famous people on slips of paper and include the names of everyone in the group. Another version of the game is to write the names of people in your ward. Each team gets 30 seconds to pull the slips of paper out of a bowl one at a time and give word clues until her teammates can guess the right name. When the group guesses it gets to keep that slip of paper. The winning team is the group who has collected the most slips of paper.

- "Human Knots." Have everyone stand shoulder to shoulder in a circle. Explain that the group will be working through a challenge to untangle a human knot. Have each person stick their left hand into the circle without touching anyone. Then have them grasp the hand of a different person who is not standing next to them. This should tangle the group. Now have them work together to untangle the knot without letting their hands go. If you have an odd number of people in the group when you grab hands the first time you will have an extra hand. When everyone sticks their second hand into the circle you will find enough hands at that time.

- "Sponge Plunge." Divide into two teams. Place a bucket and a large sponge by the first person on each team. Place an empty bucket a certain distance away from each team. At the signal, the first person dips the sponge in the water, runs to the other end, and wrings the water into the empty bucket. When the first person runs back, the next person goes. The first team to finish, wins one prize, and the team that is able to squeeze the most water in the bucket, wins another. Talk about how we are each like sponges, soaking up the kind or hurtful words of one another.

- "Tic Tock." Everyone gets a slip of paper with a word on it such as "Disney" or "Root". They have to mingle with the others in the group until they find someone else whose word works with theirs such as "Disney-land" or "Root – beer."

- "Love One Another." Have everyone sit in a big circle. One person is left in the middle and is "It." That person goes up to someone and says, "Do you love me?" The seated girl can answer "Yes" or "No." If she says "Yes" she then gives up her seat and becomes "It". If she says "No" she has to explain why such as "No, but I love everyone with blonde hair" or "everyone with red socks" at which time anyone who fits that description has to exchange places while the person in the middle tries to get one of their seats. The last person left is "It." Play until everyone has had a turn being "It."

- "Siamese Twins." Cut off one sleeve on an old T-shirt and sew it to another old T-shirt whose opposite sleeve has been cut off, making one giant T-shirt for two girls to share. Have them play games and sports together and then feed each other dessert.

- "Sink Your Teeth Into This Game." Sit in a circle and have a contest to see who can do various tasks without showing their teeth, such as snorting, laughing, talking, singing, etc. Whoever shows her teeth is out until the last player wins.

- "Staring Contest." You guessed it! See who can stare the longest without blinking or laughing.

- "Who's Who?" Write the names of famous people on slips of paper and tape them to the girls' backs. They have to mingle and ask each other questions until they can guess their identity.

- "Hug the Pot Holder." Give everyone a pot holder they must hug without using their hands. Choose someone to be the "Judge" who will tell them if they're hugging the pot holder correctly or not. The Judge has a pot on her lap. See how long it takes for them to figure out they're supposed to hug the judge!

- "Give Her A Hand." A fun game to play to get to know a new Primary presidency is for the new leaders to stand behind a table or blanket that is being held up by two of the girls. The leaders then put a hand out while the rest of their body is covered up. The rest of the girls have to ask yes or no questions to the hands, trying to guess who it is. To answer "yes" the leader gives a thumbs up and to answer "no" she gives a thumbs down or shakes her index finger.

- "Yes/No." Write the word "Yes" on one side of a paper and the word "No" on the other side. Simply ask the group questions they have to answer such as "Do you have a pet?", "Can you do a cartwheel?", "Do you like spinach?" etc. The girls will get a kick out of seeing how everyone answers the questions.

- "Pig Heaven." Tape everyone's noses up by putting a long piece of clear tape from the top of their lip to their forehead. That alone is cheap entertainment. Now have everyone take turns seeing who can do pig calls the best, snort like a pig, and sing a farm song.

- "Sticky Fingers." Tape everyone's thumb down to the palm of their hand and then have them do various tasks such as writing their name with a pencil, using chopsticks, clapping, snapping their fingers, putting a pillow in a pillow case, eating a snack, putting on a coat, etc.

- "Don't Eat Molly!" Make a board game with as many squares as there are girls. Draw a different face to represent each girl. Put a small piece of candy on each square. Have one of the girls leave the room while the other girls choose one of the faces on the board to be "It." When the girl comes back into the room she is invited to eat the small candies one at a time. When she chooses the candy that was on the "It" square all of the girls yell "Don't Eat Molly!" (or whatever the real girl's name is who is represented by that square.) The winner is the girl who can eat the most candy before choosing "It."

- "Sock Darts." Every girl is given an old, but clean sock to decorate to look like her. Fill the toe area with beans and then tie it with elastic or yarn. Have the girls take turns tossing their sock towards a target such as a hula hoop or a circle drawn by tape on the floor. You could also write points on pieces of paper and the girls earn the amount they get their sock dart closest to.

- "To Tell The Truth." Give everyone a paper to write down something amazing they have done. Choose one of the papers and have three of the girls stand in front of the group, being sure to include the one girl who really wrote the paper. Have the three girls try to convince the group that they were the one who actually did that particular thing. See if the group can guess who was telling the truth.

- "Watermelon Seed Spitting." Who doesn't love a good old-fashioned watermelon seed-spitting contest? See who can spit their seed the farthest or to a certain target on the ground. Gee, guess what you're having for refreshments?

- "Shoe Pile." Everyone takes off one of their shoes and throws it into a big pile. Then each person picks up a different shoe from the pile and finds the person it belongs to.

- "Light Sabers." Have the girls pick a partner and put their hands together, hooking them with an index finger sticking out like a light saber. The object of the game is to poke each other. Once you have been poked you sit down and the partner that's left finds a new partner until it comes down to the champion.

- "Hula Hoop Contest." See who can hula hoop the longest or craziest. Have them make up tricks they can do with the hula hoop on their arms or one foot or with a partner.

- "Shot Put Throw." Blow up a bunch of balloons. Each person gets three chances to throw the inflated balloon as far as possible. Another variation is to play on teams and play shuffleboard with balloons.

- "Cookie Dash." Divide into two teams. Place a plate with a large cookie on it and a glass of milk a certain distance from each team. Instruct teams to form a line. At the signal, the first person from each team runs to the cookie and eats it. She must not only eat the cookie but must drink the milk before running back. (Be sure to check for food allergies first.) The next person runs down quickly, eats a cookie, and drinks a glass of milk. Each person must take a turn. Have a person at each end pouring glasses of milk and replacing cookies. The first team to finish wins.

- "ZIP/ZAP/ZOP." Everyone sits in a circle and someone begins by pointing to another person in the circle and saying "ZIP!" That person then points to yet another person and says "ZAP!" That person points to another person and says "ZOP!" This continues, but the words must be said in order: ZIP, ZAP, ZOP. If someone makes a mistake and says a word out of order, that person is out of the game. Eventually, the circle dwindles to just a few people, then to only 2 people, who are staring at each other, yelling ZIP!, ZAP!, ZOP! Until one of them makes a mistake.

- "HAVE YOU EVER?" All of the girls stand in a circle. Each takes a turn asking a question, "Have you ever_____"(filling in the blank). Those who have, answer yes by walking to the center of the circle and slapping a "high five" with whoever else has done the action.

- "Water Balloon Toss." This one is always a hit. Another variation is to use raw or hard-boiled eggs. Choose partners and stand facing each other. Toss a water filled balloon to the other person. After each toss, the partners must take a step backward. The last set of partners to have an un-popped balloon wins.

- "Pile Up." Have the girls sit in a circle in chairs with a little bit of space between chairs. Have a leader in the center of the circle give directions such as "Everyone with jeans on move 3 spaces to the right" and the moves are made. Continue calling out different commands for things about who is wearing a necklace, what type of shoes people have on, the color of shirts, pony-tail, etc. Most likely the girls will end up sitting on top of each other, sometimes 4-5 deep. Teach the girls to celebrate the differences and enjoy one another.

- "Utensils." Everyone sits in a circle. One person gives a fork to the girl sitting next to her and says "This is a fork." The receiver says "A what?" and the giver repeats "A fork!" The receiver then says "Oh! A fork!" and then repeats the conversation with the girl sitting next to her. Somewhere else in the circle another girl has started a similar conversation with a spoon going in the opposite direction. Include a knife, a spatula, and whatever other utensils you want to use. The game is pretty much over when everyone is laughing.

- "Jelly Beans." Have girls guess the flavor of various jelly beans. "Jelly Belly" has great ones. Next have them design a jelly bean that reflects their personality without the other girls seeing them work. They need to color a jelly bean design on paper and then select a name and display real jelly beans that illustrate their concoction. Finally, display the jelly bean creations and see if the girls can guess who made them. Have each girl explain why she designed her jelly bean the way she did.

- "Soft Sculptures." Have a bubble blowing contest first. Then, once the gum is sufficiently soft, have each girl create a sculpture of a Primary child, CTR ring, or any other item. Put each sculpture on a 3 x 5 card and have an unbiased judge select the winner.

Web sites with ideas for more fun get-to-know-you games!
　　www.gameskidsplay.net/
　　www.funattic.com
　　www.funandgames.org
　　http://adulted.about.com/od/icebreakers/
　　http://www.eslflow.com/ICEBREAKERSreal.html
　　http://poped.org/icebreakers.html
　　http://ce.byu.edu/yp/ythconf/games/initiative.htm
　　http://www.teach-nology.com/ideas/ice_breakers/
　　http://www.geocities.com/EnchantedForest/Glade/6694/
　　　icebreak.html

Chapter Thirteen

Birthdays

There are so many ways to celebrate each child's birthday. The most important thing is to make her feel special and loved. Here are just a few ways to shine the spotlight on her, as well as some small gift ideas to let her know you care:

- Take a picture of each girl on a special "Glamour Shots" night or whenever you can get a good shot of each girl. Put a big mat on it and have each of the other Primary children write a loving message to the birthday girl on the mat. Frame it, wrap it, and present it with hugs from everyone!

- Fill a #10 size can with inexpensive items such as a CTR ring, bookmark, Articles of Faith card, treats, etc. and seal the can. Most stakes have a sealer that can be used for free.

- Make "Birthday Cakes In A Bottle" by using 1/2 pint wide mouth jars. Spray the jars with oil and fill 2/3 full with brownie batter. Bake until done. Heat up the lids in hot water while the brownies bake and then quickly place the hot lids and rings on the jar to seal. Put a small wooden spoon on top and wrap with cellophane paper when cooled, tying it with cute ribbon or raffia.

- Create a framed copy of the picture on the front of the "Faith In God" book on transparent paper over a picture of the birthday girl.

- Present a white rose and a white hankie that has her name written on it that she could take to the temple when she is old enough.

- Fill a basket with inexpensive gifts from the $1 store so that the girls can choose any item they would like on their special day. Every girl is different and this way you can appeal to a lot of different tastes and styles.

- Make a bookmark or frame with the "My Gospel Standards" or Articles of Faith written nicely, adding pressed flowers or ribbons.

- Present the birthday girl with a small Christus statue. They can be made fairly inexpensively at a local pottery store. Even better, teach the girls how to make them.

- Kidnap the birthday girl early in the morning and take her out to breakfast in her pajamas.

- Give her a bag of Hershey's candy with a note attached that says "HearShe's having a birthday."

- Make the birthday girl wear a tiara and one of those "Miss America" banners, but instead have it say "Birthday Girl" or "Primarily For Birthday Girls".

- Decorate a brown paper bag, fill it with treats, and tie it with raffia for a country look.

- Present the birthday girl with a bunch of "Good For One" home-made coupons. You could even have the other girls make a bunch of coupons in advance and they each have to offer something of themselves.

- Buy each girl a special "Birthday Journal" that she can begin keeping for herself. Each year she writes things about herself and her life so that she can see her growth.

- Invite all of the Primary children to write kind things about each other. Create a special card for each girl so that she can receive her card on her birthday with all of the thoughts previously written by the other girls.

- Make one of those giant chocolate kisses in foil for the birthday girl. (Pour melted chocolate in a funnel for the shape.) Put it on the floor in her classroom and say "We KISS the ground you walk on."

- Make a necklace that spells out her name in cute beads.

- Gather well wishes from the birthday girl's family, teachers, and friends and put them all in a pretty binder to present to her.

- Buy some clean, polished rocks and write some of her talents and qualities on each rock with a permanent marker. Present them to her in a velvet drawstring bag.

- With her parents' permission, of course, sneak into her bedroom when she's not home and decorate her room with birthday balloons or flowers.

- Put hearts all over her bedroom or front yard with a note saying she has received a "heart attack" from people who love her.

- Put wrapping paper and a bow on her bedroom door.

- Hang a giant poster at her school or home wishing her a happy birthday from all the Primary children in your ward.

- Hang a balloon from the ceiling with small notes from all the girls and leaders. When you sing happy birthday she gets to pop the balloon and get the letters.

- Fill a basket with different kinds of pretty lotions and sing her this song sung to the tune of "We Wish You A Merry Christmas":

We wish you a happy birthday
We wish you a happy birthday
We wish you a happy birthday and an awesome new year
Good lotions we bring to you and your skin
We wish you a happy birthday and an awesome new year

- Give each girl a charm bracelet when they turn eight years old. Add a special charm for each birthday, as well as other events such as baptism, completed Faith in God goals, recitals, giving talks, etc.

- Have an "Unbirthday Party" just for fun to celebrate everyone's birthday at once or just to break up the monotony of a long, cold winter. Have everyone bring either goofy presents or a nice gift under $5 to play the "White Elephant" game.

- Create a cookie bouquet to give to each girl on her special day.

- Give each birthday girl her own Primary Songbook and instructions on how to conduct songs.

- Put a picture of the birthday girl and another one of Christ between two pieces of glass and then frame. Add a quote, pressed flowers, lace, ribbon, etc.

- Give her a CD of Primary or LDS-related music. You can even e-mail the artist and request that they autograph it or sign a note to the birthday girl.

- Present her with her very own fresh rose. She may never have received one before!

- Decorate a canvas bag with the annual Primary theme written on it in fabric paint. Encourage her to bring her bag each week filled with her scriptures, "Faith In God" book, bookmark, note paper, etc.

- Have a combined monthly birthday party for all of the girls who are celebrating that month.

- Make chocolate lollipops for all of the girls celebrating birthdays that month and present them all at once.

- Show her baby picture to everyone and have them guess who they think it is. Present her with a bag of Baby Ruth candy bars.

- Give her a collection of Mormon Ad posters.

- Present her with toe socks with a "Faith in Every Footstep" note attached to remind her to have faith in God and work on her goals.

- Create a photo album by starting her first page which includes a photo of her, the Savior and a nice display of the Primary theme.

- Invite all of the girls to stand up. As you read things that describe the birthday girl tell the girls to sit down if that item does not describe them. The birthday girl will be the last one standing. Sing happy birthday to her and present her with a little gift.

- Invite the parents of the birthday girl to make cupcakes to share with the group at the Activity Day closest to her birthday. Hey, who said YOU have to do all the work?

- Write about the birthday girl and put the paper in a balloon. Have someone pop it and then guess who it is.

- Send an e-mail birthday card using free cards at www.dayspring. com which includes a nice, inspirational quote from scripture. Other free cards can be sent from:
  www.bluemountain.com
  www.123greetings.com
  www.birthdaycards.com
  www.freewebcards.com
  www.superlaugh.com

- Design a festive birthday poster that can be rolled up and stored each month. Take a picture of the birthday girl in front of the poster. Keep a copy for your ward scrapbook and present her with a copy for her scrapbook.

- Present a birthday mug, basket, or some other decorated container filled with various items in it. She then, in turn, fills it with items and presents it to the next birthday girl.

- Spotlight all of the birthday girls each month on a bulletin board or special poster, by displaying pictures and information about each girl during the month.

- Photocopy a clip art flower on to brightly colored paper and cut them out. Cut out green leaves and tape them to straws, creating flowers with a stem. Have the girls write loving messages on the back of the flowers and present the birthday girl her special bouquet. You could even photocopy a picture of the birthday girl into the center of each flower.

- Invite the birthday girl's parents to come in and talk about how great their daughter is. Limit the time to five minutes. They can show baby pictures and brag about all of her accomplishments. Be careful to not let this spotlight time turn into an uncomfortable competition and be especially sensitive to the girls who do not have parents who could present a birthday message.

- Design Primary "money" with clip art and award the birthday girl with some birthday bucks that she could cash in at the "Activity Days Store" (a box with miscellaneous items to choose from). "Activity Days Dollars" could also be earned each time the girls pass off an Article of Faith or accomplish another goal in their Faith in God booklet.

- Create a flower or candy lei for the birthday girl. Add notes to the birthday girl from each of the girls to be placed in between the flowers or candy.
- Be sure to have your Primary secretary mail the birthday girl a special card signed by the Primary presidency!

Chapter Fourteen

Finding Lost Sheep: Less Active Girls

Be sensitive to each girl's situation. Primary children are often eager to attend Activity Day, but sometimes their parents are resistant or simply unable to get their daughter to certain events. Some of the following ideas might be just what one girl needs to feel welcome and desire to reactivate while it may offend another. Sometimes you can gently press and other times you have to step back and allow more time and space.

As a leader you have been given the right to receive inspiration for your calling. Ask Heavenly Father what approach to take since He knows and loves each daughter more than anyone.

* "L.A.M.B." Prepare a LAMB (Less Active Members Back) event for all of the girls. Decorate your room with lots of lambs and pictures of the Savior with sheep. Prepare a paper lamb or a nice craft one that provides the name, phone number, address and birthday of each less active girl in your ward that will then be given to an active girl. There is a lovely Church movie called "Feed My Sheep" that could be shown. Talk about the parable of the lost sheep, Christ's admonition to "Feed my sheep", how the Savior shepherds us and how we can be like shepherds as well in finding His "lost sheep." Explain that each active girl will be a shepherd to the assigned girl for a designated amount of time and can do several things: invite her "lamb" to church on Sunday and to Primary activities, offer to help with transportation if

necessary, call her to chat, send her friendly notes, remember her on her birthday, and visit her if appropriate. Give each active girl a little lamb with a note saying "Ewe can make a difference." Make little sheep out of cotton, marshmallows or pom poms.

- Call the less active girls, letting them know they were missed.

- Bring them handouts or announcements they missed by not attending Activity Days or Primary meetings.

- Ask the Ward Council to help.

- Plan a surprise party for each less active girl.

- Fill a basket with simple things like candy, quotes, bookmark, picture of Christ, Pass-along cards, etc. Have your group deliver them to the less active girls.

- Get a picture of each less active girl and paste it onto the back of an empty milk carton with the words "MISSING" in large black letters above the picture and "Have you seen me?" below. Serve milk and cookies at an activity to see if the girls even notice the pictures. Talk about how it's important to put names with faces and that when we pray for the less active we need to know who we're really including in those prayers.

- "Attendance Bingo" Make a special Bingo card for each girl and stamp it or put a Primary sticker on each square when she attends Church on Sundays or an Activity Day. Award prizes for attendance. Sometimes all girls need is a little extra motivation.

- Hide a bead somewhere in the room where you meet. At the beginning of the meeting show the girls a box of beads and tell them that you want to make something special with them. Look at the beads and note that one is missing. Set out in search of it. The girls will naturally join in. When the missing bead is found thank the girls for their help. Tell them that the beads represent them. Whose bead was lost? Identify the names of the girls who are less active. What you want to make with the "beads" is a loving Primary. Invite the girls to make a bracelet and pick out one bead to remind them every time they see it to think of the less active girls.

- Invite each girl to bring a stuffed animal that represents them and share why they chose the one they did. Attach a name tag to each animal. Each week set up as many chairs as there are young girls in your Activity Days group. Whenever a girl isn't there set her stuffed animal on the chair to represent her. That way everyone can really "see" who isn't there. You could also use little lambs for each of the girls.

- Encourage the Primary presidency to make in-home visits to all of the girls, bringing them a little treat. Sing a song, chat, share a short devotional, or just "hang" with them for a few minutes.

- Create a life-size Primary girl out of cardboard and talk about her different body parts, pointing out such things as how her HEAD should be filled with the words of Christ, her EYES should focus on her goals, her HEART should feel love towards others, her ARMS should reach out with service, etc. Talk about how some BODY is missing in your class and how we can use those body parts to help.

- Make appointments to do "bedroom inspections" at each of the girls' homes. Wear a white glove as if you're testing for dust. Tell them something is terribly wrong and that they are missing something...Church! Invite them to attend, give them a calendar of events and a little treat, handout, picture of the Savior, etc.

- Taste different kinds of grapes and talk about how we have the privilege and responsibility to work in the Lord's vineyard. Share the allegory of the Olive Tree in the Book of Mormon or how our faith can grow like a seed into a plant.

- Watch a part of the movie "Charlotte's Web" or read the story. Talk about how strong a spider's web is. Throw a ball of black yarn to one girl in the circle and tell what she contributes to your class. She then throws the yarn to another girl, holding a piece of the yarn in order to create the look of a web. Talk about how strong your class is because of all the girls' talents and love. Decorate cupcakes with spider web frosting.

- Sing the Primary song "I Am Like A Star Shining Brightly" and find out which stars are missing in your class. Focus on how each star (Primary child) shines and makes the class brighter.

- Create a monthly report that records what types of contact were made with each girl. That will serve as helpful information as try to determine which approach is successful with each girl.
- Recruit the help of the less active girl's Home Teacher and the mother's Visiting Teacher (if there are some that are going to the home.)
- Find out if the less active girls are receiving a copy of *The Friend* magazine. If not, consider buying her a subscription or leaving last month's issue at her doorstep when you are through with your copy.
- Teach the girls to know the details about all of the girls: WHO is not attending, WHY they aren't able to come, and HOW we can help them.
- Visit the less active girls at their athletic tournaments or musical performances. Your presence and support can say more than your words.

Ideas for "love letters" and "we miss you" gifts

- Attach a note to a can of soda that says "We soda-lighted that you're in our Primary!"
- Box of crayons: "Add COLOR to your life! Join us next week in Primary!"
- Popcorn: "We just popped by to see how you are." or "Feel free to POP into Primary any time!"
- Popcorn ball: "We think you'll have a BALL at Primary with us!"
- Dollar Store Calculator: "We COUNTING on you to join us next week for our next Activity Day!"
- Can of Rootbeer: "We're rooting for you and hope your day is going well!"
- Loaf of bread: "No matter how you slice it, we miss seeing you at Primary!"
- Basket of bath items or treats: "When you feel like a basket case, just remember we love you!"

- Cute little lamb: "Ewe are missed!"
- Pace Picante Sauce: "Take a break and slow your PACE. We miss your face!"
- Angel pin, ornament, decoration: "We think you're an ANGEL and when you join us at Primary it's just HEAVENLY!"
- Oven mitt with treats: "We have to adMIT you're a great girl!"
- Toy airplane: "It's PLANE to see you mean a lot to us in Primary!"
- Cookies: "We think you're a real smart COOKIE!"
- Bananas: "We go BANANAS when we don't get to see you at Activity Days!"
- Squeeze-It juice box and Hershey's kisses: "Here's a SQUEEZE and a KISS so you'll know you are missed!"
- Bear-shaped honey: "Hi HONEY! We think you are BEARY sweet!"
- Gummy Bears: "We can't BEAR it when you're not with us at Activity Days!"
- Sweet Tarts: "We think you're a real SWEETART!"
- Sparklers: "You add SPARKLE to our Primary! We hope to see you again shining brightly again soon at Activity Days!"
- Emory board/nail file: "It's ROUGH when we don't see you for awhile!"
- Musical note or CD: "Just a NOTE to let you know we're thinking of you!"
- Mug with hot chocolate mix: "Just sending you a chocolate hug in a mug!"
- Can of soup or dry soup mix: "We think you're SOUPer!"
- Heart candy: "You're in our mind and our HEART!"
- Smiley stickers: "We missed your smile at Activity Day!"
- Donuts: "DONUT you know that we miss you when you're not with us?!"
- Grater & cheese: "We think you're GRATE!"
- Flowers: "If friends were flowers we'd pick you!"

- Lifesaver candy: "Be a LIFESAVER! Come help us have fun at next week's Activity Day!"
- Lightbulb, Highlighter pen: "You LIGHT up our class when you come to Primary Activity Day!"
- Frozen pizza: "We think you're the TOPS with lots of PIZZAz!"
- Aim Toothpaste or a target & arrows: "We hope you'll AIM to be with us at our next Activity Day!"
- Pretty tray with goodies: "We TRAYsure your friendship."
- Nuts: "We're NUTS about you!" or "We have some fun to SHELL out at Primary this week!" or "In a NUTSHELL, we miss you!"
- Starburst candy: "You're a STAR in our Primary class!"
- Mug with hot chocolate: "To our friend who is so dear, we wish you this big cup of cheer!"
- Body Glitter: "You just SPARKLE when you come to Activity Days!"
- Gum: "By GUM, we miss you when you're not at Primary!" or "We hope you CHEWS to go to Activity Day this week!"
- Bouncy ball or gumball: "Primary is a BALL when you're with us!"
- Cupcake or cake: "We think you're just great! You take the CAKE!"
- Mounds candy bar: "Our Activity Day next week would be MOUNDS of fun if you were there!"
- Toffee or brittle: "Any way you break it, we miss you!"
- Candy: "Everything is SWEETer when you're with us!"
- Bread: "We KNEAD to see you at Primary again so we can RISE to our potential!"
- Key or paper cut into the shape of a key: "You are the KEY to our having a great Activity Day !"
- Toy watch: "WATCH the time, don't be late. Remember in Primary you really rate!" or "We'll be WATCHING for you in Primary next week!"
- Leaf: "We beLEAF you will love our next Activity Day!"

- Basket of fresh strawberries: "You're BERRY special to our Primary class!"

- Picture of a radio or TV: "TUNE in for next week's Activity Day! Enjoy the gospel in STEREO!"

- Lion stuffed animal or picture: "No LION, we missed you this week at Activity Day!"

- Yarn: "We're YARN'n to see you again in Primary!"

- Toy sailboat or picture of the ocean: "Long time no SEA! We missed you!"

- Grapes: "We miss you a BUNCH!"

- Stuffed dog: "DOGgonit! We miss you in Primary!"

- Balloon: "We'll be DEFLATED if you don't join us next week for Activity Day!"

- Doll: "We think you're just a DOLL!"

Chapter Fifteen

Christmas Ideas

The Christmas season is magical and allows for special activities that bind and create lasting memories like no other time of year. It's also an extremely busy time of year, so remember to be mindful of the hectic schedule your leaders, girls and their families have. Be careful to not over plan during the holidays, but to choose activities that are meaningful and draw the girls closer to the Savior and the "reason for the season."

Activities

- Work with your Ward Activity Chairman and have the girls help plan a special nativity show by inviting everyone in the ward to bring their nativity sets to display. The girls could decorate the cultural hall or another room and pass out special invitations or flyers to invite the community. This could become a huge community event or just a fun tradition for your ward members to enjoy. Provide a written card next to each display identifying what country the crèche is from or whose it is. One ward painted backdrops to go behind the displays, played Christmas music and had people walk by Christmas paintings in between the nativity sets for a longer show. It helps the girls (and all of us) to focus on the birth of Christ rather than get caught up in the commercial distractions.

- Read the parable of the White Stocking (found online) and have the girls make and decorate them to use at home with their families.

- Create a "Bethlehem Experience." This would be a great ward activity because it requires a lot of work, but can be such a powerful experience. Turn your cultural hall into Bethlehem, complete with village shops, Roman soldiers, an inn, and a stable. Guests visit booths, taste samples of food of the day, learn how to make a craft, hear music, fill out a census for taxing, pet sheep, etc.

- Learn about the nature and symbolism of the gifts that were brought by the wise men and show samples. Talk about things that we love, need, and want. Discuss gift-giving customs and have the girls prepare a gift they could give the Savior by creating a special box where they and their families would write a goal they will meet the next year or a bad habit they will "give away."

- Present a lesson about JOY: J= Jesus, O=Others, Y=Yourself. Decorate the room with Christmas decorations that say JOY. Have the girls create two ornaments with the word JOY on it.

- Have a "Kris Kringle Mingle." Share Christmas stories and provide copies for each girl to put in a special Christmas binder she can then share with her family. Some families read one story each night while a candle burns down to another mark as a type of advent. For tons of stories check out:
  www.allthingschristmas.com/stories.html
  www.joyfulheart.com/christmas/
  www.infostarbase.com/tnr/xmas/
  www.inspirationalstories.com/christmas-1.html
  www.santaville.tripod.com/stories.html

- This is a fun way to do a gift exchange. Read a story that has the word RIGHT or LEFT in it or make one up. Everyone holds a gift in their hands and then moves it either to the right or left as the story is being read. They get to open the gift that ends up in their hands at the end of the story. For an example of a story check out www.homemakingcottage.com/holidays/cmas/gift_exchange1.htm

- Everyone brings a favorite Christmas decoration to show and then tells a favorite Christmas story. Top off the night by eating everyone's favorite Christmas goody.

- In November have the girls create an advent calendar for their family to use at home. You can use chocolates or candy strung together, a paper chain with scriptures written on each link, felt picture of a stable with 24 different nativity pieces to add each day, a tree calendar where you add ornaments each day, and more! Check out some of the many different ways to make one at:

  www.ehow.com/how_11216_make-advent-calendar.html
  www.familycrafts.about.com/od/adventcalendars/
  www.creativekidsathome.com/activities/activity_14.shtml
  www.kidsdomain.com/craft/advent1.html

- If your Stake or Ward sponsors a Giving Tree project then you could provide gifts to needy families as a Primary group. If no such project exists, then you could be the ones to start it! Get a list of needy children from your Bishop or Stake President and coordinate donations by hanging information about each recipient on a paper ornament on a "Giving Tree." Information should not include a name, but instead the age, sex, clothing size, and possibly the wish of each child. When someone wants to buy a gift for that person he takes the ornament to remind himself of his commitment and then fills out a donor card with his own contact information and puts it into a specially decorated box. That way you can remind him, collect the item, send a thank you card, etc.

- A few weeks before your chosen activity day, pass out brown lunch sacks to all of the young women to decorate at home. The girls will then fill their bags with whatever gifts they would like to give. On your activity night or Christmas party every girl who brings a filled, decorated bag then gets to select another bag to take home. Every bag will be different so its contents will be a fun surprise. The giver remains anonymous unless you want each girl to include a little note inside with a special Christmas message that identifies who she is. You might want to suggest a maximum budget to be spent on the contents.

- One month before the Christmas activity night have the girls pick each other's names out of a hat to determine who will be a "Secret Sister" for whom. During the next few weeks the girls can do all kinds of anonymous service and make little gifts for the girl or leader whose name she picked out of the hat. You may want to establish certain guidelines that limit the dollar amount of spending to encourage the girls to be more creative and so it won't be a financial burden. At the Christmas party all of the Secret Sisters will reveal themselves to each other. Often times there will be girls who go all out while others don't do very much. Be sure that it is a voluntary experience so that only the young women who really get excited about this idea will participate, while others who don't want to do it can gracefully slip out.

- Give each girl a collection of Primary stickers for her to put on her calendar for the new year to remind her what dates Activity Days will be held as well as quarterly Primary activities and special events. The girls can design their own calendars or you could provide copies of photos that have been taken of the girls during the past year.

- In all your preparations for the holidays, help the girls focus on the birth of Christ and encourage a more spiritual celebration during the holidays. Make costumes for families to recreate the Nativity story in the scriptures.

- Have the girls make special Christmas bookmarks that identify the story of Christ's birth and can be placed in their families' scriptures during the holidays.

- If your ward boundaries include your church building you could either begin or end at the building. Hopefully you'll get lucky and find some girls who live close enough to each other that you could walk or have a short drive to each house after each course. You can have separate houses for hors'deourves, soup, salad, entrée, and dessert. You may want to limit house visits to just three homes if they're located farther away. If none of the sisters live close enough to each other to make it practical you could host a traveling dinner by using and decorating different rooms in your church building.

- Help the girls create a photo calendar they can present to their families as a gift for Christmas.

- Create an Activity Day of "Christmas Stations." This could be a progressive event where each activity is held in a different home or else in a different room of your Church building.

  Station 1 – Christmas stories
  Station 2 – Musical presentation
  Station 3 – Christmas candy-making demonstration
  Station 4 – Gift ideas
  Station 5 – Focus on Christ, sing Christmas carols

- Find out ahead of time how many girls and leaders would like to participate in an ornament exchange. Everyone makes the same number of home-made ornaments and then exchanges them with the others in the group. Everyone shares a favorite Christmas memory or talks about any sentimental value they have with certain ornaments.

- Host a "Christmas Around the World" activity where you focus on international décor, food, music and learning. Invite returned missionaries to tell about the foreign country where they served, and display items. Don't forget to include the United States!

- Choose several homes or neighborhoods the girls could visit together and sing a selection of Christmas carols. Bring plates of cookies to give away and have everyone wear Christmas colored clothing and Santa hats. Give copies of music selections so the girls can take them home and plan a caroling evening with their families in their own neighborhoods. Have them invent new words to familiar tunes and call them "Cracked Carols."

- Offer a fun workshop full of mini-classes on how to make attractive gift baskets, cookie bouquets, inexpensive gift ideas, gifts from the kitchen, card making, how to ship presents so they don't break in the mail, home-made wrapping paper ideas, how to show gratitude, teachers' gift ideas, and thank you card ideas. Be sure to offer a lesson that all of the girls can attend that encourages them to focus their holiday efforts on Christ.

- Sew holiday pillow-cases for the whole year by using fabric with holiday designs.

- Have the girls make a wooden nativity set they could keep for their future children and families.

- Drive around to see the Christmas lights together. Talk about how Jesus is the light of the world and how the girls can share their light with others.

- Tell the girls they're going to go Christmas caroling. Let them sing at a few houses, and then when you stop at another house have someone dressed as a shepherd or Mary say "Shhh, the baby is sleeping." Then they escort everyone to an area where a living nativity is set up. Take turns reading about the Savior's birth from the scriptures or have someone do a special presentation about the true meaning of Christmas.

- Kidnap the girls early in the morning by singing Christmas carols to them and taking them to a special breakfast in someone's home. Be sure to arrange this with the parents ahead of time! Only pajamas are allowed. Share Christmas stories, sing carols, make and/or exchange gifts.

- "Sub For Santa" or "Elfing." Arrange special service projects.

- Festival of trees. Attend a local festival or create your own! Invite families in the ward to enter a decorated, themed tree in a competition. Coordinate with your Ward Activity Chairman to use the trees as decorations for the Ward Christmas party.

- Make special decorations that represent stories and people from the Book of Mormon to hang on a Christmas tree such as Lehi's "Tree of Life."

- "Snowflake Attack." Cut out a bunch of snowflakes to hang on someone's door anonymously and leave a plate of goodies too! The girls will get the thrill of playing ding-dong-ditch, but they'll really be spreading Christmas cheer!

- Help your Ward Activity Director make backdrops, props, Santa gift bags, table decorations, or anything else that is needed for the Ward Christmas party.

- Have a white elephant gift party. Everyone brings a wrapped gift and sits in a circle. Draw numbers. The first person chooses any gift to open. The second person can "steal" that gift or opened a new one. Keep going until everyone has had a turn. It's fun to make the rule that no gift can be "stolen" more than three times.

- If you've been taking pictures all year long you could have a scrapbooking party, slide show presentation, or photo swap.

- Invite the girls to bring all of their unfinished crafts and other projects and finally finish working on them!

- Choose a family to do the "Twelve Days of Christmas" to by dropping off little Christmas items at their house each night. You could also wrap 12 items in a basket with a note telling them to only open one item each night. Include a scripture reference for each day.

- Have a cookie exchange.

- Make decorations for the Ward or Stake New Year's party.

- Make gifts for the Stake Presidency, High Councilmen, and Bishopric for all of their service during the past year.

- "Are you part of the INN crowd or one of the stable few?" When the girls walk into the room drape Biblical fabric swatches around them and have them sit on cushions on the floor. Cover tables with burlap, beads, oil lamps, gords, etc. to create a feeling of being in Bethlehem. Talk about what life must have been like for a young girl back then.

Gift ideas

Here are some ideas for the leaders as well as the girls to learn how to make gifts for others.

* "In His Footsteps." Tie fuzzy socks with a pretty ribbon and attach the following quote by Thomas S. Monson "What will you and I give for Christmas this year? Let us in our lives give to our Lord and Savior the gift of gratitude by living His teachings and following in His footsteps. It was said of Him that He went about doing good. As we do likewise, the Christmas spirit will be ours."

- Make little mangers, using a small block of wood, straw or Spanish moss for hay, and small plastic baby that's wrapped in linen or felt. Use a hot glue gun to attach a piece of curled wire to the wood block and add a dangling star to the other end, over the baby Jesus.

- Decoupage a picture of Christ on an ornament and attach this note:

    As you hang this ornament on the tree, remember
    the man who walked the shores of Galilee.

- Make a "People Feeder." Buy inexpensive chicken feeders and fill with small candies.
- Make Candy Cane Bath salts by placing one cup of Epsom salt and ½ cup sea salt into a Ziploc baggie. Add 3 drops of peppermint oil and squish around. In a second container mix 1 cup Epsom Salt, ½ cup sea salt and 3 drops of red food coloring. Layer the red and white salt mixtures in a clear bottle and decorate with ribbon and a candy cane!
- Create an ornament by attaching this poem to a card that has a nail on it:

    ## "THE NAIL"
    It's Christmas time at our house
    and we are putting up the tree.
    I wish I could find one simple way
    to remember Christ's gift to me.
    Some little sign or symbol
    to show friends stopping by
    The little babe was born one day
    But he really came to die.
    Some symbol of his nail pierced hands,
    the blood He shed for you and me...
    What if I hung a simple nail
    upon my Christmas tree?
    A crimson bow tied 'round the nail
    as His blood flowed down so free
    to save each person from their sin
    and redeem us for all eternity.
    I know it was His love for us
    that held Him to that tree
    but when I see this simple nail
    I know He died for me.

    AUTHOR UNKNOWN

- Tie ribbon to a Christmas cookie cutter and attach a note that reads "In order for a COOKIE to come out right you need to use a pattern. We, too, in order to turn out right, need to use a PATTERN—The Savior's."

- Help the girls to "clearly see Christ" by using clear, glass ornaments that you can insert a picture of Christ inside.

- Place a picture of Christ and an inspiring poem or quote in between two pieces of glass. You can use two inexpensive frames for the glass, using one of the frames to hold it all together. Add ribbon, lace, pressed flowers or whatever else you would like, using only a few glue dots to affix each item to the glass.

- Attach a note to a can of soda that says, "We soda-lighted to wish you a Merry Christmas!"

- Put a ribbon around a bath, dish, or hand towel and a note that reads "

    May the ABSORBING Spirit of the season:

    BLOT out problems,

    SOAK up sorrows,

    WIPE AWAY difficulties,

- Using clean, dry soup cans or those big food storage cans, paint holiday designs on the outside and fill with treats.

- Have the girls decorate bookmarks with their photo on it. Laminate them to give as Christmas gifts to friends and family.

- Nativity Set: Drop off one piece of a nativity set each night until the set is complete. Include a scripture reference with a note about that particular piece and the part it plays in the Christmas story.

- Create "Magic Reindeer Dust" by mixing some dry oatmeal with glitter in a small baggie tied with a ribbon. Include directions for the user:

    On Christmas Eve night, when it's dark and still
    And Santa is on his way.
    Sprinkle this magic food outside
    And it will guide his sleigh.
    Rudolph will smell the oatmeal

As they hurry across the sky
And the sparkle of the glitter
Is sure to catch his eye.
So say your prayers and jump in bed
As softly as a mouse,
so Santa and the reindeer
Can visit every house!

- Wrap a little box or block of wood to look like a present and attach this note:

"This is a very special gift
that you can never see.
The reason it's so special is
It's just for you from me.
Whenever you are lonely
Or even feeling blue,
You only have to hold this gift
And know I think of you.
You never can unwrap it.
Please keep the ribbon tied.
Just hold the box close to your heart
It's filled with love inside!"

- Make fabric boxes that could be filled with candy or sweet love notes. Cut holiday fabric into squares or rectangles with pinking shears. Dip fabric in melted wax with tongs and quickly place over a mold such as a loaf pan or bowl that has been lightly sprayed with oil. Crease the corners so they will fold nicely. Let sit until cool and stiff. Cut a piece of cardboard to fit the bottom, fill with treats and wrap with cellophane or tissue and a ribbon.

- Give the girls a hand . . . literally. Roll out skin-colored polymer clay and then trace the shape of your hand with a pencil, cutting with an exacto knife. On the bottom write the name and date in pen, pencil or a thin permanent marker. Shape hands upside down over a custard dish and cook for about 10 minutes in a 275 degree oven. After cooling, varnish with two coats. Put treats or anything in the opened hand and wrap!

- Box of Christmas lights or flashlight: "May your Christmas be radiant and bright!"
- Put this cute poem on a store bought chocolate bar:

  A day or two ago,
  I thought I'd make a treat
  For all my special friends-
  A Christmas gift to eat.
  My intentions were top notch,
  but my schedule would not budge,
  Hence, here's this year's edition
  Of homemade Christmas fudge!

- Make a CD for each girl with next year's Primary Sacrament program music on it.
- Find Nativity or other ornaments at www.autom.com
- Create brown antlers out of pipe cleaners to root beer bottles. Add little eyes and a red nose for Rudolph. Make flavored oils and vinegars and put them in decorative bottles. There are tons of great recipes and instructions on the Internet.
- Strainer: "We couldn't reSTRAIN ourselves from wishing you a Merry Christmas!"
- Eggnog: "Have an udderly MOOvelous Christmas!"
- Hershey's kisses in a wire whisk: "We WHISK you a Merry Kissmass!"
- Whoppers: "We hope you have a WHOPPER of a Christmas!"
- Cookie Dough: "We think you're a smart COOKIE! Here's a little extra DOUGH for Christmas!"
- Bell: "With each chime of this festive bell may a Christmas wish come true, and bring you peace and happiness to last the whole year through!"
- Ice scraper & brush: "May you learn from the SCRAPES of this past year and allow the Savior's love to BRUSH away your tears."
- "Last Year's Snowman": A small carrot with two buttons floating in a jar filled with water.

- Bubble gum or bubble bath: "May your holidays BUBBLE OVER with the spirit of Christ."
- Music CD: "May the sounds of Christmas put a song of love in your heart!"
- Package of sewing needles: You're just sew sharp! Merry Christmas!"
- Pencils and notepads: "Merry Christmas from our PAD to yours!"
- Make cinnamon dough ornaments by mixing 1 cup of apple sauce with 1 cup of cinnamon. Add 1 teaspoon of both nutmeg and cloves. Roll out like cookie dough and cut into shapes, remembering to put a little hole towards the top to tie a ribbon through. Dry at room temperature for about a week, turning them over every other day.
- Can of Sprite: "May your Christmas be merry and SPRITE!"
- Jar of Jam: "We hope your holidays are JAM packed full of good cheer and the spirit of Christ!" Or "We just wanted to SPREAD some holiday cheer and wish you a Merry Christmas!"
- Angel ornament, pin, decoration: "We think you're just an ANGEL! May your Christmas be HEAVENLY!" Or "May you always have an ANGEL by your side."
- Box of gloves: "This is the HANDiest Christmas present we could find!"
- Frozen pizza: "Warm up to a great holiday season, TOPPED with Christmas cheer and lots of PIZZAz!"
- Heart ornament or pin: "May the joy and love you give away come back to you on Christmas Day!"
- Measuring Cup or spoons: "Wishing you a joy beyond MEASURE!"
- Candle: "May your days be happy, your heart be light, your Christmas merry and your New Year bright!"
- Grate and cheese: "We don't want to sound CHEESY, but we hope your Christmas is just GRATE!"
- Can of soup or dry soup mix: "We hope your Christmas is SOUPer!"

- Homemade frozen rolls: "Here's a little holiday treat. Rise and bake. It can't be beat! Warm fresh rolls just for you. Top with butter, that's all you do! Warm holiday greetings from us to you."

- Spiced apple cider, Wassail, or Christmas spices: "We just wanted to SPICE up your holidays!"

- Jolly Ranchers: "Have a JOLLY Christmas!"

- Joy dishwashing soap: "My your Christmas be full of JOY."

- Bag of microwave popcorn: "We thought for hours what to give you for Christmas and then suddenly this idea POPPED into our heads! Merry Christmas!" or

  "Christmas comes but once each year,
  And always keeps us hopping!
  Running around here and there
  Christmas wishes dropping. So,
  When your feet are tired and sore,
  And you feel you should be stopping,
  Sit right down and have a rest
  While this corn is popping!"

- Paint holiday designs and add ribbon to sisal door mats for a festive and practical gift for the home.

- Check out www.organizedchristmas.com for tons of fun ideas!

- Take a roll of toilet paper and some heavy craft wire. Curl the wire loosely and thread through the toilet paper roll. Join the ends and attach a bow and pine, attaching this silly poem:

  "What better place to hang a wreath,
  than on the door that gives relief?
  Merry Christmas!"

Chapter Sixteen

Fun Traditions

Traditions create a feeling of unity and security. Some of the following ideas might not work in your ward or branch, but they may get you thinking about what special traditions you can begin to create continuity and wonderful memories in your Primary.

- Invite other wards or the entire stake to share a Faith In God activity together annually. It could include a craft, short lesson, refreshments, guest speaker, stations the girls rotate through to pass off various achievements, or a service project.

- Create special mailboxes for each girl. You could use an actual mailbox or assign a hanging file folder for each girl in a box. Put little love notes, announcements for future events and handouts in. Open up the mailbox at every meeting and pass out everyone's mail. At a quick glance the leaders can see whose folder is full to see who hasn't been coming very much lately. The girls could also take turns being responsible for putting a surprise in the folders once a month. Keep some stationery and pens near the box to encourage the girls to write kind notes to each other or leave anonymous "love" letters to one another.

- In a world full of terrible news headlines, it's nice to hear some good news! Once a month, have the girls share with the group their good news. It can be anything from getting an A on a test to giving a talk in Church. Be sure to cheer and applaud their successes and good news. Set the timer for only 1 or 2 minutes and when the bell rings everyone knows it's time for the lesson or activity to begin.

- Design a Primary wall. Mission presidents hang pictures of all of their missionaries on one large wall where they can constantly be reminded of them. Make a board like that with pictures of all the Primary children for your Bishop to hang in his office or in the Primary room.

- Make prayer sticks. Each girl writes her name on a popsickle stick and decorates it however she'd like. Of course, you can use something more clever and cute than a popsickle stick! Whenever you ask one of the girls to pray have her select a prayer stick out of a specially decorated can to include that girl's name in her prayer. The girls become more mindful of each other's needs and a sense of unity is developed when they hear other people praying for them!

- Decorate the Bishopric's door every month to remind them how important they are to the Primary. Put pictures of the girls on cut-out hearts for February, write the names of the girls on pumpkins for Thanksgiving, you get the idea. That simple act of surprise service will also draw the hearts of the children to their priesthood leaders.

- Take lots of photos of the girls at every activity so that at the end of each year or for the graduating eleven year olds you can present a special scrapbook for them.

- Create an Activity Day Girls Choir. If you spend a few minutes singing each time you gather, you'll be able to polish a song fairly quickly that could be sung as a musical number in Sacrament Meeting or even Primary. Try to incorporate the girls' instrumental talents as well.

- Begin a Primary Newsletter. If your ward or Primary presidency isn't already creating a special newsletter, you could create your own. Present your girls with a newsletter each month or quarterly with pictures of past activities, articles about the girls, fun polls, helpful information, announcements for upcoming events, poems the girls have written, suggestions for cool web sites to check out, birthdays, leaders' phone numbers, and spotlights on girls who accomplish their goals or just need a little extra attention that time. Fill the pages with whatever interests your girls and encourage them to submit their own artwork, stories and photos. It doesn't have to be an enormous project; even a two-sided sheet of paper where you slobber all over the girls would be great!

- Establish a "New To You Table." Set out a table where the girls could bring any of their unwanted items from home and anyone is free to take whatever they want. The items that still remain at the end of the activity could be delivered to Goodwill, Deseret Industries, Vietnam Vets, or any other organization of your choosing. You could also deliver items to your local Spanish branch or whatever special needs branch you have in your area. You can have the girls bring random items each month or designate a different theme each month such as perfume, toiletries, clothing, etc. This could be a one-time activity or held every month.

- Set out a "S.O.S Table." S.O.S stands for Seek Out Service. Each month or quarter, one or two organizations are spotlighted so the girls can get ideas for service projects they can get involved in with their families or to pass off a service goal. This is an opportunity to introduce the girls to ways they can become more involved in their community and reach out to others. You can provide pamphlets or flyers with a contact phone number so the girls can follow through with their interest. Organizations you might want to introduce to the girls could include: American Kidney Foundation, Second Harvest, American Cancer Society, Candy Stripers, United Way, Toys for Tots, local nursing homes they can visit or perform in, local hospitals they can volunteer in, etc.

- Incorporate "Secret Sisters" during the holidays or summer months to break up the routine a little.

- The recipes for the refreshments served during the month could be given to the girls to add to their collection. A special binder or box could be given to all of the girls where they can keep all of the recipes together to remember their time in Primary. The girls could also submit their favorite family recipes to create a ward cookbook.

- Have the girls create a Family Home Evening lesson for their families each month. Each packet could include visual aids, a recipe for the refreshments, songs that coordinate with the selected theme, and even a refrigerator magnet with a scripture. The girls could choose what topic they would like taught or you could provide stories and visual aids for them to color based on the topics in their Faith in God booklet.

- Control "chit chat" by creating a special time for it. The girls always have so much to say one another each time and it's often frustrating to have to keep telling them to be quiet during the lesson. When you first gather together, set the timer and allow the girls to chit chat as fast as they can until the timer goes off. Once they hear the bell they know their time is up and now it's the leader's turn to talk.

- Establish "Gathering Time." The Cub Scouts include a "gathering time" activity at the beginning of their meetings as the children slowly meander into the room. It could be a craft, puzzle, writing assignment or art project that gives the prompt arrivals something to do while waiting for the stragglers to join in.

- Prepare a "Quilting Corner." It would be fun to have a quilt set up somewhere each month that the girls could work on while they visit with one another. Quilts could be ongoing projects, made as gifts from your ward Primary for new babies, graduating seniors, new brides, families in need in the ward or as an international humanitarian project. The girls could be encouraged to work for a few minutes each week as a gathering activity while you wait for everyone to arrive and begin your official activity. Learning how to quilt could be passed off as one of their "Developing Talents" goals.

- Have a "Sister Spotlight." Each month a different girl is spotlighted and given a little gift. She stands in front of the group while someone tells all about her favorite things, her accomplishments and talents, and why she is so special to the Primary program in your ward. You could also tell the group all about her and have the others guess who they think it is and then present her to the group.

- Keep a Primary Scrapbook. Be sure to take lots of pictures of the girls each time. Encourage your Primary presidency to begin keeping a scrapbook or create one just for Activity Days. Teaching the girls how to design attractive scrapbook pages could be one of their "Developing Talents" goals as you all work on a special book together. This could be a big activity once a year or quarterly. It could also be a gathering activity each week to give the early-birds something to do while you all wait for the others to arrive.

- Put together a Primary Photo Directory. Digital cameras make putting together a photo directory a snap! An updated directory could be printed every six months or yearly. The directory could include phone numbers, addresses and e-mail addresses of the girls and leaders. Although this idea encourages increased communication among all those in the Primary program, it could also be the source of security problems for the safety of your girls if placed in the wrong hands. You would need to stress the importance of the girls' safety before handing out such a list and would need to get parental permission beforehand.

- Door prizes are fun to use to help solve any problems you might be having with Activity Days to reward positive behavior. For example, if your girls have a tendency to straggle in late every week you could award door prizes to all the girls who are there on time. If you want to encourage missionary work with the girls you could offer a little prize to each girl who brings a friend each month. Door prizes could also be offered randomly to add a little excitement. Prizes don't have to cost much and can even be donated by local vendors. All you have to do is ask!

- Present a Book of Mormon Challenge. Each week or month the girls could be challenged to share a Book of Mormon with a non-member friend. Have the girls give a short report on her experience. Have a contest with the Cub Scouts to see who can give away the most copies.

- Create a "Lunch Bunch." Once a quarter the Primary leaders could meet for lunch with the girls at their school. Give an award for the "Most tasty brown bag" or other goofy categories.

- A friendship basket could be filled and presented each month to a girl whose name has been drawn out of a hat. The recipient then brings the basket filled with new items for the next month's Friendship Basket. The basket should not be a financial burden, but an opportunity to simply express friendship and sisterhood.

- Serve a special cake once a month to celebrate all of the girls and leaders who have a birthday that month. It might be kind of fun to include birthdays of current apostles, past prophets or other people in Church History.

- Send "Monthly Missionary Messages." A table could be set out once a month with stationery, note cards, markers, etc. so that the girls could write letters of encouragement to the missionaries who are serving from the ward. All of the letters could then be mailed either separately or together in a special care package from the Primary. Similar packages of cards and letters could be mailed to any ward members serving in the military or college students away for the school year.

- Set up a "Get To Know You Table." Once a year invite all of the girls to bring a few items to put on a table that describe themselves and their interests so that all of the other girls can get to know them a little better.

- Everyone who arrives at activity night with another girl gets a little "Carpool Award" prize. Carpooling encourages the girls to bond, invite and remind each other to attend, in addition to saving gas money and the environment!

- Have a countdown for the next temple that will be built and dedicated, especially if there is one near you. Do special activities to prepare or find Pen Pals from a ward or branch in that area you can write to.

- Have each girl choose a silk flower that best represents her. Create a bouquet of all the girls and use it as a centerpiece at special events.

- Bring a goodie jar with candy or non-food treats that the girls can reach into when they've brought their scriptures to class each time.

- You could call this a "Meet Me Basket" or "Sisterhood of the Traveling Basket." Each week someone fills a basket with things that describe her. She presents the basket to the class and writes about her likes and dislikes in a special binder that remains in the basket.

- Begin an annual tradition called the "Crystal Apple" or "Teacher Appreciation Golden Apple." Each girl invites a teacher, coach or adult who has made an impact on her life to a special dinner. This can be an annual event that really encourages reaching out into the community.

- Being extremely careful to protect the identities of your girls, you might consider creating a ward Activity Days web site where you could post announcements, maps, links, etc. You would need to get parental consent before posting any photos and NEVER reveal addresses or phone numbers. For free space, visit these websites: www.myfamily.com, www.homestead.com, or www.geocities.com.

- Become pen pals with girls in another ward or branch far away. Join a discussion board for Primary leaders and you're sure to find someone in another state or country who would like to swap letters, ideas, and care packages with your girls.

- Get together during a General Conference session to watch it together. Play Conference Bingo. To help the girls prepare for conference you could play "Name That Apostle" and teach the girls a little bit about each of the men in the Quorum of the Twelve. Another fun twist to learning about the apostles is to make playing cards of them by making 4 copies of each picture and play "FISHers of Men" (like Go Fish where they have to collect four of the same pictures to make a "book.")

- Each month have the girls collect various items for a women's shelter. For example, during the month of May you could remind them to bring toiletry items to Activity Days or in a cold, winter month they could bring socks or mittens. The constant reminder and repetition will turn their hearts to others.

- Have the girls take turns decorating a Primary bulletin board for your room.

- Hold a "Linger Longer." The Primary could begin a tradition in your ward to hold a monthly after-Church supper, complete with awards for best dishes.

- Award "Caught Being Good" coupons to girls when you want to reinforce good behavior (attendance, language, kindness, service, etc). They can turn in their coupon to the Bishop who will have a special basket of treats waiting for them (which you provide him with).

- Invite a "Sister Friendly" to attend your Activity Day once a month or quarter to share stories or play games that incorporate *The Friend* magazine. With parental permission, take pictures of the girls or drawings the girls have made to submit to the magazine in the "Our Creative Friends" section. Show the girls how to make the recipes from the Kitchen Krafts section. You could also learn a song that has been printed in *The Friend* or do the mazes and games to get them excited about reading their issue at home.

Chapter Seventeen

Websites

A word of caution about doing Internet searches for ideas. If you enter "Girls" into a search engine you could get suggestions for links to all kinds of horrible pornographic web sites. You must type in LDS, Primary, or Activity Days, and even then, look at the description of the site before you click on it! Once you innocently click onto a porn site they will have your e-mail address and will send you disgusting e-mails until you have to shut down your account! Unfortunately, I speak from experience! Oh, that the world were as clean and pure as our sweet children.

- www.lds.org
  The official web site of the Church of Jesus Christ of Latter-day Saints. Click on "Serving in the Church" then choose "Primary" and then "Primary Activity Days." This should be your first stop on the Information Superhighway!
- www.ldscatalog.com
  Purchase official Church items.
- www.ldsactivitydays.com
  Fun ideas shared by many other Primary workers.
- www.primarypage.com fun ideas
- www.theideadoor.com/Primary.html
  Tons of fun ideas, clip art, charts
- www.christysclipart.com
  Free clip art for every occasion

Some of the following sites specifically have Primary ideas, but many have ideas that could be adapted for Activity Days.

- www.jennysmith.net
  A wonderful resource for everything!

- www.promoms.org/activitease.htm
  General Primary helps

- www.youngwomen.faithweb.com
  Has a helpful Primary page

- www.lds.about.com/od/ldsprimary/
  Lesson ideas, games, puzzles, word searches, downloads

- www.eprimary.dk/index_uk.htm
  Games, downloads, clip art, lessons, music and more!

- www.deseretbook.com/mormon-life/
  Tons of teaching resources. Scroll through the list to see the ones that focus more on children.

- www.of-worth.com/cc/
  Poetry, stories, quotes, ideas

- www.mormonchic.com/gospel/achievement.asp
  Ideas based on the Achievement Days program

- www.achievementdays.com
  Tons of ideas based on the Achievement Days program

- www.ldsfiles.com/dir/Church_Organizations/Primary
  Lots of links and resources

- www.lightplanet.com/mormons/primary/index.htm
  Overall Primary ideas, activity ideas based on the Achievement Days program

- www.songsoftheheart.com/primary.html
  New free songs perfect for Primary!

- www.angelfire.com/ma/lissaannapage/primary.html
  Poems, quotes, recipes

- www.geocities.com/meadfamily/primaryhelps.htm
  General Primary ideas, links

- www.edhelper.com/bingo.htm
  Build your own puzzles, worksheets and games

- www.ldstoday.com/home/level2/PrimaryIdeas.php
  Overall Primary ideas
- www.sugardoodle.net
  Cute ideas for lessons
- www.bellaonline.com/subjects/1992.asp
  Links to ideas for children
- www.debanae.net
  Mostly Young Women things, but some free Primary clip art and products
- www.familyfun.com
  Great magazine with tons of ideas for children and families
- www.homeandholidays.com
  Recipes, crafts, patterns, miscellaneous ideas
- www.jenmagazine.com
  Fun, free, online magazine for LDS girls
- www.dltk-holidays.com
  Tons of fun holiday ideas and celebrations you've never heard of with crafts and activities
- www.kidsites.com/sites-fun/girls.htm
  Links to sites young girls love!

Craft ideas

Girls love to make crafts. Below are web sites with zillions of project ideas you could tweak to fit a gospel context.

- www.makingfriends.com
- www.creativekidsathome.com
- www.gsleaders.org/files/crafts.htm
- www.allcrafts.net/kids.htm
- www.mailjust4me.com/crafts/girlcrafts.htm
- www.parentingteens.about.com/od/crafts/
- www.achildswork.com/Girly_Stuff.htm
- www.rubyglen.com/crafts.htm
- www.kids.discovery.com/fansites/tradingspaceskids/crafts/crafts.html

- www.childfun.com
- www.dcrafts.com/kidscraftsp1.htm
- www.geocities.com/Athens/1850/
- www.michaels.com/kids/kcproject.html
- www.fibrecraft.com
- www.deltacrafts.com
- www.craftsforkids.miningco.com/library/bltrashtr.htm

LDS search engines

- www.ldsresources.com
- www.lds.mycityport.com
- www.lds.npl.com
- www.ldsindex.org/resources
- www.zionsearch.com
- www.ldslibrary.com
- www.ldsabout.com
- www.mormon-lds-gateway.org
- www.ldstoday.com
- www.mormonlinks.com
- www.mormonfind.com
- www.ldsvoices.com
- www.users.olynet.com/mkathj/lds.html
- www.mormonhaven.com/miscel.htm

Merchandise

- www.ldscatalog.com
  Order Church materials
- www.littlestreamrecords.com
  Primary songs and more
- www.ldsfiles.com/link/?1024689378
  LDS games, puzzles, teaching tools
- www.quiettimeinc.com
  Books, games, visual aids

- www.jeannigould.com
  Beautiful LDS music for girls
- www.softlore.com
  Memorizing scriptures software
- www.ldsounds.com
  LDS music and merchandise
- www.ldsaudio.com
  LDS music, books
- www.primarytogo.com
  Games, free downloads
- www.seagullbook.com
  LDS books, music, merchandise
- www.orientaltrading.com
  Inexpensive and fun items for any occasion
- www.my-personalized-gifts.com
  LDS jewelry
- www.ctrcreations.com
  Dozens of LDS products
- www.lds-yw.com/html/primary_suggestions.html
  Primary stickers
- www.ldscharms.com
  LDS jewelry
- www.ldschurchgifts.com
  LDS items
- www.deseretbook.com
  LDS books, music, merchandise
- www.ctr-ring.com
  CTR rings
- www.greatlengths.com
  Modest clothing
- www.mormon-t-shirts.com
  LDS apparel
- www.lds-store.com
  LDS jewelry, apparel

Clip art

I'm thankful for talented artists who share their wonderful creations with me, since I have trouble drawing decent stick people! Here are links to some of those generous artists who share their talents:

- http://lds.mycityport.com/
- www.christysclipart.com
- http://www.graphicgarden.com/
- www.debanae.net
- http://designca.com/lds/
- http://clip-art-free.be/news
- www.coloringbookfun.com
- www.lds.mooseberrygraphics.com
- www.stums.org/closet/html/index.html
- http://www.oneil.com.au/lds/pictures.html
- http://lds.about.com/library/gallery/clipart/blclipart_gallery_subindex.htm
- www.free-clip-art.net
- www.ldsfiles.com/clipart
- www.coloring.ws/coloring.html
- www.apples4theteacher.com
- www.happytulip.com/catalog/coloring.php
- www.kidsdomain.com/clip/
- http://www.lds.org/gospellibrary/pdfmagazine/0,7779,594-7-1-2001,00.html#

Discussion groups

I recommend that you join a Yahoo Group. It's free to join and you'll meet some of the nicest people around! People share helpful ideas and tips in a real-time setting. You can receive the e-mails individually or as a daily digest. Some groups are more active than others so the quantity of e-mails will vary. There is no reason to reinvent the wheel when another great Activity Day leader has already done it out there somewhere!

Yahoo groups:

- ldsactivitydays
- StakePrimary
- PrimaryPage
- PrimaryST
- Lds_CSL
- craftingLDS
- PriPres
- LDSsharing
- CluelessLDSPrimaryPresidents
- ldsprimarykids
- www.latter-dayvillage.com
- www.mormonchic.com/forum

Blogs

- www.happyjellybeans.blogspot.com
- www.primary-teacher-uk.co.uk

About the Author

Trina Bates Boice grew up in sunny California and later braved the cold and snow at Brigham Young University where she earned two Bachelor's degrees. While there she competed on the BYU Speech & Debate team, and BYU Ballroom Dance Team. She was President of the National Honor Society Phi Eta Sigma and ASBYU Secretary of Student Community Services.

Trina also studied at the University of Salamanca in Spain and later returned to serve a full-time mission to Madrid, Spain for the Church of Jesus Christ of Latter-day Saints. She earned a Master's degree from California College for Health Sciences.

She worked as a Legislative Assistant for a Congressman in Washington D.C. and wrote a column called "The Boice Box" for a local newspaper in Georgia where she lived for 15 years. She has a real estate license, travel agent license, a Black Belt in Tae Kwon Do, and helps her husband, Tom, with their real estate appraisal and investment companies.

Trina was honored in November 2004 as George Bush's "Points of Light Volunteer" and also received the President's Lifetime Volunteer Service award. She was the "2004 Honor Young Mother of the Year" for the state of California. She and Tom live in beautiful Carlsbad with their four wonderful sons.

Trina is a host of Roots Television. See her presenataions at **www.rootstelevision.com/vlogs/climbing-family-trees.html**

Trina can be contacted through her personal website at **www.boicebox.com**